Getting Started
in Metals

The Getting Started In Series

Getting Started in Stocks by Alvin D. Hall

Getting Started in Futures, Second Edition,
by Todd Lofton

Getting Started in Options, Second Edition,
by Michael C. Thomsett

Getting Started in Bonds by Michael C. Thomsett

Getting Started in Mutual Funds by Alan Lavine

Getting Started in Metals by Jeffrey Nichols

Getting Started
in Metals

Jeffrey Nichols

JOHN WILEY & SONS, INC.

New York ▪ Chichester ▪ Brisbane ▪ Toronto ▪ Singapore

Library of Congress Cataloging-in-Publication Data:

Nichols, Jeffrey A.
    Getting started in metals / Jeffrey Nichols.
        p.   cm.
    ISBN 0-471-55557-6 (pbk. : acid-free paper)
    1. Metal trade.   2. Metal trade—Finance.   3. Investments.
    4. Commodity exchanges.   5. Stock options.   I. Title.
    HG6047.M48N53   1995
    332.63—dc20   94-23712

Printed in the United States of America

10 9 8 7 6 5 4 3 2 1

Contents

v

PART 1

AN INTRODUCTION TO METALS

CHAPTER 1

Why Metals?

In all of my years as an economist, researcher, investor, businessman, and entrepreneur, I've never found an investment arena that offers as much intellectual challenge and as much potential financial reward as metals. Metals—copper, aluminum, nickel, platinum, and gold, just to name a few—are the backbone of the world economy. These and other metals are essential components in the capital equipment necessary for the functioning of any modern economy. Metals are key ingredients in many of the items we take for granted—autos, airplanes, telephones, computers, electronics equipment, household appliances, and even ballpoint pens.

CHANGE EQUALS OPPORTUNITY FOR INVESTORS

The 1990s has already been and will continue to be a period of immense economic change. The fall of communism in the former Soviet Union and Eastern Europe and the emergence of market-oriented economies have enormous consequences for both the supply and demand of many metals. But this is only one of many ongoing shifts in the global economy with significant implications for metals markets. Others include:

- increasing numbers of Asian economies which are major industrial powers,
- the new economic dynamism in China,
- the establishment of democratic governments in Latin America and the renewed growth in output and income throughout the region,
- the continued plight of much of Africa and, in particular, the political changes which have taken place recently in South Africa.

Moreover, after the global economic slow-down/recession of the early 1990s, the world economy is now enjoying renewed expansion. These fundamental changes—and the prospect of moderate economic growth in the mature industrial democracies—have uneven but generally positive implications for metals prices over the medium to long-term.

The premise of this book is that metals investing offers even the beginning investor significant profit opportunities. Meanwhile, the more savvy investor who has an understanding of how changes in the global economy may affect each metal market should be able to profit whether prices are rising or falling.

Metals investing need not be complex or difficult. This book will be your guide, telling you what you need to know to start investing successfully in metals. You don't have to be a beginning investor to benefit from the information and guidelines presented in the following chapters. Whether you are a sophisticated individual investor or a professional fund manager, you will find ideas in this book that will help you improve your performance and enhance your returns.

Although I believe that global economic and political trends will be generally bullish for metals prices through the end of this decade, the purpose of this book is not to predict or forecast the ups and downs in prices for each of the metals discussed. Nor is it my intention to make specific investment recommendations. In a period of rapid economic transition, smart investors must be capable of continually reassessing the fundamentals of each metal market in light of the changing global economic landscape.

DO IT YOURSELF

My goal is to provide you with a framework for assessing metals markets and price prospects on your own—so that your short-term and long-term investment strategies need never be out of date. For each metal presented in this book, there is a section titled: *Getting Started*. It will give you a foundation for understanding and analyzing each market—where does the metal come from, what is it used for, how to analyze the supply and demand *fundamentals*, and what factors drive the price.

fundamentals: refer to the actual supply and demand for a metal or commodity as well as the factors that have a direct bearing on trends in supply and demand.

Investors can choose among a wide range of metals and minerals beginning with aluminum and ending with zirconium. One industry reference book lists about 65 metals and minerals in its table of contents. *Getting Started in Metals* does not propose to cover such a wide gamut. Instead, I've restricted the discussion to a small number of major metals that are easily accessible to the average investor through physical ownership, equities, futures, or options.

Throughout this book, certain words appear in italic type. Definitions of these words appear in the glossary which is intended to serve as a permanent desk reference for the investor. Usually, these words are highlighted in italics the first time they appear—but occasionally they may be highlighted again to remind the reader that additional information on its meaning is available. In addition, a brief definition of some words will appear in the outside margin the first time they are used, but all appear in the glossary.

Just the mention of the word metals to many investors conjures up images of speculators and boiler rooms—but metals investing can be sane and sensible. You *can* speculate in metals by trading commodity futures—and for some investors this may be a legitimate approach. But there are *less speculative* ways to participate in this investment sector that are appropriate for even the faint at heart.

It would be misleading to suggest that one investment strategy is right for everybody. Individual investors—depending on their relative wealth, income, financial obligations, age, investment sophistication, and willingness to accept risk—will have differing approaches to and goals from a metals investment program. Similarly, metals investing can be conservative and risk-averse with a long-term perspective—or it can be aggressive and risk-taking with a short-term trading orientation.

Another objective of this book is to help each investor develop the approach that is right for his or her specific circumstances. A conservative investor might buy a mining company stock on the New York Stock Exchange as a long-term investment. In contrast, an aggressive investor might trade *futures contracts* on a commodity *futures exchange*. Indeed, the vehicles available for metals investors range from mining company equities on both domestic and foreign stock exchanges to purchasing and holding physical metals to trading futures and options contracts.

A selection of the readily available investment vehicles for each metal will be presented so that you can choose the one that's right for you. All of the metals included in this book are readily accessible to the average investor through one or another conventional investment instrument. Later in *Getting Started in Metals*, I'll discuss the basics of investing in the major investment categories and markets—mining and metals equities, U.S. futures markets, the *London Metal Exchange*, *options* on equities and futures, and for precious metals buying coins and *bullion*.

futures exchange: a membership association organized to facilitate the trading of futures contracts.

London Metal Exchange: the physical market in London, England—established in 1882—where a number of metals, including lead, copper, tin, aluminum,—are traded. Also known as the LME, metals prices set by free and open trading on this exchange often serve as benchmark prices around the world.

CHAPTER 2

How to Analyze Metals Markets

Thorough market analysis is a prerequisite to profitable investing and speculating in metals. Fortunately, the economics of metals markets are simpler than most economists admit. And, for the average investor, common sense and firsthand observation of U.S. and worldwide business trends should be the starting point. Moreover, a watchful eye on technological and other trends that may affect consumption of metals often can provide the basis for the right investment decision.

Remember, the underlying principal of market economics is that *price is a function of supply and demand*—and, when analyzing metals markets, we are also interested in supply and demand. An investor must first understand the recent historical and prospective trends in both supply and demand. I always look for markets where total supply will likely grow more slowly than total industrial demand. Slow growth in supply (or declining supply) and more rapid growth in industry demand most often point to a rising price.

secondary supply:
metal that is recovered and recycled from junked metal-bearing items, such as old printed circuit boards, copper plumbing, or scrapped automobiles.

primary supply:
refers to metal that enters the market directly from mining activities.

concentrate: mine ore or other metal-containing material which has been treated to remove certain unwanted constituents prior to refining to produce metal of high purity.

smelter: a company or industrial complex that processes metal-bearing ores or scrap.

We will discuss some basic questions you should be able to answer before investing in any metal market.

SUPPLY PROSPECTS

What are the major sources of supply? In what countries is the bulk of mine production located? Is mining activity in any of these countries currently or potentially affected by local political, economic, or labor problems? For example, at times in the past, copper prices have sometimes rallied sharply because of strikes and labor disruptions in Chile. The future of gold and platinum is already being influenced by political developments in South Africa.

In addition to mine production, *scrap* recovery (that is the recycling of junked metal-bearing items such as aluminum cans or copper electrical wire and contacts) is an important source of metal to the market. In the jargon of market analysts, scrap is often referred to as *secondary supply* while mine production is *primary supply.* In some markets, scrap flows are very sensitive to the metal's price with higher prices encouraging more recycling. In other markets, scrap may never amount to much or it may be a regular and significant component of supply.

In many metals markets—copper, lead, and zinc, for example—mine output is not in marketable form. These mines produce a semi-finished product called *concentrate* which must be smelted and/or refined before it can be sold as usable metal. Hence, the supply of marketable metal may be dependent not only on mining activity (and secondary supply) but on *smelter* and *refiner* capacity and output.

INDUSTRIAL USAGE

What are the recent and prospective trends on the demand side? How will business conditions and other factors influence offtake in the future? Metals consumption is usually related to trends in industrial production and business activity in the major consuming economies. But changes in technology, environmental regulations, consumer preferences, relative costs, and other factors can also have a significant influence on demand trends. Are any of these developments leading to substitution to or away from the use of one metal or another? Is the intensity of metals usage in any important application changing?

For example, the introduction of auto *catalytic converters* (which require unleaded gasoline) beginning in the 1970s and the drive to remove the metal from paint erased two major end-use markets for lead. At the same time, the catalytic converter created a major new use for platinum and palladium. The rise in silver prices in 1980 led to efforts by the photographic film industry, the largest consuming sector, to reduce the intensity of usage, contributing to the subsequent long-term bear market for silver. Developments of this sort can have a dramatic influence on metals price trends—and they may be as visible to the informed individual investor as they are to the professional market analyst.

As with mine production, geography and regional trends in consumption also can be important. One important development, in recent years, has been the emergence of several Asian nations as important manufacturing centers. This has made them consumers of raw materials—and the rise in

refiner or **refinery:** a company or industrial complex that processes raw metals in order to separate the constituents of alloys and/or to remove impurities.

approved refiner: a commercial refiner whose branded bars (or product in other forms) are accepted as good delivery by one or another metals or futures exchange.

catalytic converters: the pollution control devices used in the exhaust system of most automobiles. Platinum and palladium serve as the catalysts in the chemical conversion of harmful auto emissions to nontoxic gases.

business activity and, hence, personal income has also created new markets for finished consumer and capital goods. Rapid industrialization of many previously backward or developing countries is now a key factor in the analysis of metals markets and the forecasting of metals prices.

FACTORING IN THE EAST BLOC

Over the next decade, developments in the former Soviet Union, other former East Bloc countries, and China undoubtedly will also have an important bearing on metals markets and prices. These countries are both big miners and big consumers of many metals. The breakdown in the economies of Russia and the other members of the former Soviet Republic is already disrupting mine production of gold, platinum, nickel, and other metals with probable medium- to long-term consequences. In the short run, however, the need for hard currency led to accelerated sales of many metals in 1990 and 1991, inflating world supplies and depressing prices early in the decade.

Industrial production in the former Soviet Union has also collapsed, leading to a sharp drop in domestic metal consumption, freeing up additional supplies for export or reducing import demand for metals which are not mined in sufficient quantities. Over the years, depending on the pace of economic recovery and reconstruction, demand for many metals will revive—and eventually could surpass previous requirements.

China is another "wild card" in the supply/demand equation for many metals. The country's huge population and its relatively rapid pace of economic growth and industrialization makes the People's Republic of China a very important consumer of many metals. Imports and sometimes big buying binges have occasionally in the past had a profound influence on world metals markets and prices. Sometimes when prices are rising—for copper, as an example—one need look no further than China for the explanation.

THE BOTTOM LINE

The bottom line for metal market analysts is the *surplus* or *deficit*. By definition, a surplus arises during a given time period when total supplies entering the market from mine production, scrap, and net sales exceed industrial consumption. The result is a buildup in stocks or inventories held by dealers, refiners, speculators, or other investors. At other times, total supplies may be insufficient to satisfy current consumption and the market is in deficit. The gap between industrial demand and current supply is met by drawing down stocks or inventories.

    Professional metals analysts often measure estimated worldwide stocks in terms of the number of weeks of consumption that can be supported by these inventories. As a do-it-yourself analyst, you might do the same thing by simply dividing annual consumption by 52—and then dividing your estimate of stocks by this quotient.

    Sometimes these stocks are known and visible in the sense that they appear in exchange warehouses and are reported regularly in published statistics.

surplus: in commodity market fundamental analysis, refers to the excess of total supply over industrial or commercial noninvestment demand.

deficit: refers to a situation in a commodity market where supplies are insufficient to satisfy industrial noninvestment demand.

But sometimes these stocks are held by dealers or speculators around the world and are invisible to statisticians and market analysts. In an accounting sense, the surplus (or deficit) during a given time period is equal to the rise (or fall) in market stocks. We can only infer the magnitude of a market surplus (or deficit), based on estimated supply and demand trends. However, changes—up or down—in reported stocks held in exchange-related warehouses are sometimes indicative of a market's supply/demand balance.

Throughout this book, when presenting annual statistics on supply and demand for the various metals, I have tried to adhere to a fairly uniform presentation. For each metal, a statistical table presents the components of supply and industrial consumption. Adjustments are made to reflect East Bloc imports and exports. The bottom line, "Changes in Stocks," represents the market surplus (if positive) or deficit (if negative).

EXPECTATIONS VERSUS REALITY

A growing surplus is sometimes a precursor of price weakness. Conversely, a deficit may suggest future price strength. But what often matters as much as the actual market balance—and deficit/surplus situation—are expectations among traders, speculators, investors, and other market participants. Expectations of a tightening balance and a rising deficit may prompt speculative buying that pushes prices higher. Conversely, expectations of a surplus may encourage inventory reduction by industrial users, refiners, and dealers as well as short sales by speculators which all combine to push prices lower.

Expectations may be as important as Reality.

Thus, expectations may be as important as reality. The savvy investor will be just as interested in gauging the mood of the market and the consensus of expectations as in correctly anticipating the actual direction of supply and demand.

Gauging mood of the market (ie expectations) + Supply + Demand.

PART 2

BASE METALS

CHAPTER 3

Copper

C opper has long been a favorite vehicle for metals investors and speculators. Indeed, it is one
of the most accessible to the investor with a variety
of mining companies offering equity opportunities
and futures contracts and options on the *Commodity Exchange Inc.* (*COMEX*) providing more aggressive and leveraged vehicles for copper investors and
speculators. Trading on the *London Metal Exchange*
is still another possibility for the copper investor.
In addition to accessibility, copper has long been
popular among investors because it is among the
best-known and most visible of metals—both in the
sense of its widespread use and the availability of
information, data, and research.

**Commodity
Exchange Inc.,
(COMEX):** the
world's leading
gold and silver
futures market
where contracts
promising future
delivery of metal
are traded in a
public "open
outcry" forum.

COPPER USES

Investor interest in copper arises, in part, from its
widespread use in so many items that we come in
contact with on a daily basis: electronics goods and
electrical motors, telephones, computers, plumbing,
air conditioning, household appliances, automobiles, and so on. Although substitution by plastics
and fiber optics has long been seen to retard the

*Autos + Homes
Largest consumer
of copper -*

19

increased use of copper, consumer demand for all sorts of household and personal items requiring electrical controls and wiring has been the more dominant trend.

Many analysts believe that worldwide copper consumption could grow by 1.5 percent to 2.5 percent or more per year through the end of the decade. Several factors are contributing to this expected continuing long-term growth in copper demand.

In the mature industrial nations, consumers are increasingly fond of labor-saving devices that are dependent on electrical controls, computer chips, and motors. As a result, the average home built today in the United States will have roughly twice the electrical capacity as a house constructed 10 years ago. Similarly, today's automobile is apt to have electrical motors controlling power seats, power windows, remote controlled mirrors, and so on.

Table 3.1. Copper Supply and Demand Balance (thousands of metric tons)

	1988	1989	1990	1991	1992	1993
Mine production	6,721	7,139	7,213	7,396	7,370	7,500
Scrap and other refined production	1,253	1,194	1,252	1,129	1,465	1,515
Total refined production	7,974	8,333	8,465	8,525	8,835	9,015
East Bloc exports	248	233	320	351	575	525
Total Refined Supply	**8,182**	**8,566**	**8,785**	**8,876**	**9,410**	**9,540**
Total refined consumption	8,190	8,637	8,761	8,969	9,030	9,020
East Block imports	97	86	67	39	250	300
Total Refined Demand	**8,287**	**8,763**	**8,828**	**9,008**	**9,280**	**9,320**
Change in stocks	−105	−197	−43	−132	130	220

In addition, data processing and telecommunications are continuing to grow rapidly. Although personal computers, fax machines, telephones, and so on do not use a great deal of copper per unit, the number of units is expanding exponentially. Each item has power cords and/or connecting wires made of copper. Some years ago, it was predicted that fiber optics would displace the use of copper in the telecommunications industry. But fiber optics are now a net plus for copper consumption since more metal is being consumed in devices at each end of the fiber optics link than is being displaced by the cable itself.

The emergence of newly industrialized economies in Asia and Latin America, the growing middle class of consumers in many of these countries, and stronger demand in some of the developing nations are all prospectively bullish trends for copper. The potential for growth in copper consumption is greatest in the developing and newly industrialized countries where the intensity of usage is starting from a very low base relative to the mature industrial economies. Today, countries like Korea, Taiwan, Singapore, and Thailand are important consumers of copper.

China, too, is often seen in the marketplace as a huge buyer. As with many other metals, buying and selling by Chinese trading companies is often cited for otherwise inexplicable movements in the price of copper. In the past few years, the country has emerged as a significant net importer of this metal—and many observers believe that China will continue to be a big copper consumer in the years to come with positive implications for this market and the

China may have imported some 200,000–300,000 metric tons /yr in early 1990s.

metal's price. Indeed, observers believe that China may have imported some 200,000 to 300,000 metric tons per year in the early 1990s.

COPPER SOURCES

Although the United States is the single largest producer of copper, the top 10 mining countries include Chile, Zaire, Zambia, Peru, South Africa, Papua New Guinea, Indonesia, and the Philippines—all countries with risky political, business, and labor environments. During the late 1980s and early 1990s, a variety of unrelated supply disruptions from one country to the next constrained a much-predicted expansion in output and contributed to the firmness in copper prices even during the 1991–1992 recession and world business slowdown.

These supply disruptions principally in Latin America and Africa demonstrate the unpredictability and potential year-to-year volatility in copper supply. The chances seem to favor continuing periodic supply disruptions—related to strikes and labor unrest, local politics, fuel shortages, technical or operating problems, and natural disasters—simply because so much production is centered in countries prone to these sorts of problems. However, investors must realize that if the world copper mining and refining industry operated at close to full capacity for a year or two without any major disruptions, a rapid expansion in supply could be a surprisingly sharp price depressant.

One factor not well appreciated is the potential for the AIDS epidemic to disrupt mining in a number of African nations where large percentages of the local populations and mining work forces are

AIDS Factor

Table 3.2. Copper Mine Production—The Top Producers (thousands of metric tons)

	1988	1989	1990	1991	1992
United States	1,417	1,498	1,587	1,634	1,615
Chile	1,451	1,609	1,588	1,814	1,900
Canada	777	723	794	798	770
Zaire	465	441	356	291	175
Zambia	476	510	496	412	425
Australia	238	295	327	320	310
Mexico	279	249	291	267	275
Peru	298	364	318	375	360
South Africa	192	197	197	193	190
Philippines	218	193	182	148	120
Papua New Guinea	219	204	170	205	205
Indonesia	126	149	170	212	290
Portugal	5	104	160	157	150

believed to be infected with the deadly virus. Unfortunately, this could have implications for the production of copper and other metals from this region during the middle to late 1990s.

AIDS factor on other metals ?

In addition to mine production, the recycling of old scrap—from discarded electronics and telecommunications equipment, junked copper tubes and pipes, and other copper-bearing items—contributes a significant quantity of metal to the market each year. The component of supply arising from recycling is often designated *refined secondary production.* Total refined production, that is, all of the copper that is available to the market, is the sum of refined mine production plus refined secondary production plus East Bloc exports into the world market.

Both newly mined ore as well as old scrap must be refined before it is available in the market to satisfy copper-using industries. Supply depends not solely on mining and recycling activities but also upon the available capacity at smelters and refiners. During 1991 and 1992, copper prices were underpinned by an inability of copper smelters to process all of the available material from mines and secondary sources. This bottleneck disappeared in late 1992 with the addition of smelter capacity from the former Soviet Union as well as expansions at a number of western facilities. Importantly, additional capacity is anticipated to come on stream during the next few years. During the middle to late 1990s, smelting and refinery capacity will be sufficient to meet the expected levels of mine and scrap supply as well as anticipated demand.

THE MARKET BALANCE

Every year from 1984 through 1991, the copper market has been in deficit. In other words, demand exceeded supply and the needs of consumers could be fully satisfied only through a continuing rundown in warehouse stocks and inventories. During those years, about 1.5 million tons of copper were consumed out of existing aboveground stocks. As a result of this market imbalance, the price of copper rose from around $0.60 per pound in the middle 1980s to a high point near $1.60 per pound in late 1988.

In 1992, reflecting previous years of production growth, additional smelter capacity, and a weaker economic environment, the copper market moved into surplus with supplies exceeding demand as can be seen on Table 3.1. As a result, prices moved back down below $1.00 per pound.

With mine output expected to grow by at least 2 percent to 3 percent per year during the mid-1990s, price prospects are very much dependent on economic growth and the related demand for copper. The United States accounts for about 25 percent of world copper consumption while Western Europe and Japan account for 35 percent and 16 percent, respectively. In the latter two regions, copper consumption actually fell in 1992 to 1993, reflecting poor business conditions. Once recovery is well underway, copper demand in each region could grow by 2 percent to 5 percent per year during the remainder of the decade. Meanwhile, in Latin America and Asia, growth in copper use could be more robust—but these regions account for less than a quarter of total copper consumption so their impact on tonnage will be less pronounced.

Still shortage of copper 7/95.

CHAPTER 4

Lead

L ead has long been spurned by investors who remember the health and environment-related
drive to purge the metal from a number of tradi-
tional end uses—as an additive in gasoline, in building paint, and chemicals, for example. But while the
metal's negative image persists, the negative impact
of substitution away from lead on demand for the
metal had largely run its course by the beginning
of the 1990s. To be sure, lead does not have exciting
growth markets or supply uncertainties. But, however unexciting, the metal does have a fairly reliable
base level of demand and modest growth prospects.

LEAD USES

The principal use of lead today—accounting for
about 62 percent of total demand—is for batteries,
mostly for automobiles and other vehicles. Thus,
the pattern of demand from one year to the next depends importantly on: (1) the number of new vehicles manufactured around the world, (2) the
average size and electrical requirements of these vehicles (larger and longer lasting batteries use more
lead), and (3) the need for replacement batteries for

Batteries for Automobiles + other vehicles

27

(handwritten margin notes: "Auto Batteries", "1", "80% of battery sales for replacement", "more")

the existing fleet of vehicles. Battery life is, in turn, closely related to usage as well as weather. Harsh winters and hot summers strain vehicular batteries and shorten life—cold winters because of the difficulty in starting engines, hot summers because of the use of air conditioning.

In the United States, more than 80 percent of battery sales are for the replacement market. World-wide, the average is probably closer to 70 percent or 75 percent. Thus, close to 45 percent of lead demand each year is related to the replacement battery market which is a function of the existing vehicle population rather than the current vehicle production. Importantly, this means that a significant share of annual lead demand is less dependent on current economic circumstances and business conditions around the world. Investors need to be aware, however, that if the auto industry ever finds a substitute for lead batteries, the consequences on the metal's price could be disastrous.

Table 4.1. Lead Supply and Demand Balance (thousands of metric tons)

	1988	1989	1990	1991	1992
Mine production	2,317	2,255	2,341	2,488	2,503
Primary refined production	2,304	2,216	2,079	2,055	2,135
Secondary refined production	2,122	2,288	2,290	2,325	2,375
Total Refined Production	**4,416**	**4,504**	**4,369**	**4,380**	**4,510**
Net exports to East Bloc	45	30	−80	−75	−70
Total Refined Supply	**4,371**	**4,474**	**4,449**	**4,455**	**4,580**
Total Refined Demand	**4,368**	**4,526**	**4,438**	**4,395**	**4,540**
Change in stocks	3	−52	11	60	40

The next most important use of lead, accounting for about 13 percent of annual demand, is in the chemical industry. This includes lead pigments for paints; as a stabilizer in polyvinyl chloride for use in piping, guttering, and window frames; and in glass both for lead crystals as well as for light bulbs and television/video screens. Because of the health risks, the metal's use in paints has been greatly curtailed—but it is still used in the yellow pigments for road markings and signs and in the corrosion-resistant paints used on suspension bridges.

Other less important uses are in rolled sheeting used by the construction industry (principally in the United Kingdom) for roofing and flashing, cable sheathing because of its corrosion resistance, and a variety of miscellaneous applications.

LEAD SOURCES

For the most part, lead is mined as a coproduct or byproduct of other metals, particularly zinc but also silver, copper, and some minor metals. Thus, the prospects for the primary supply of lead depends in large measure on the markets and prices for these other metals.

Lead, along with zinc, is mined in many countries around the world—and there is ample capacity to increase output in response to increased demand and higher prices for these two metals. It also means that the lead market is not as vulnerable as many other metals where production is concentrated in a small number of countries, some of which may not be reliable producers. In recent years, about 65 percent to 70 percent of lead mine output derives from the industrialized countries.

Table 4.2.   Lead Mine Production—Top Ten Producers (thousands of metric tons)

	1989	1990	1991
Australia	481	540	560
United States	419	460	530
Canada	275	230	300
Peru	192	180	190
Mexico	163	180	180
South Africa	102	105	105
Sweden	82	90	90
Yugoslavia	79	80	85
Morocco	65	70	70
Spain	62	60	60

Mine production is equaled in importance by secondary supply or scrap recovery. Most lead scrap is recovered from the recycling of junked auto and truck batteries. Auto repair shops typically collect used batteries when they install new ones—so this component of supply is dependent on the replacement market for batteries. As a result, lead supply is typically less vulnerable to disruptions in mine production in one country or another, the sort of problem that often has given other metals prices a surprise boost.

THE MARKET BALANCE

Since 1980, annual surpluses in some years have more or less offset annual deficits in other years. Moreover, visible stocks held by producers, con-

sumers, metal merchants, and at London Metal Exchange warehouses have followed an erratic but
generally declining long-term trend. Should this
downtrend continue, prices could be expected to
rise gradually over the decade.

CHAPTER 5

Zinc

Zinc, because of its importance in both the auto and housing industries, is particularly sensitive to the U.S. and world business cycles. Because of the nature of its end uses, many consumers are unaware of the metal's presence in many products. In addition, zinc *alloys*—principally *brass* and *bronze* (which combine the metal with copper and sometimes other metals) have important uses. Investors can own zinc through a number of mining equities, but most often this requires exposure to lead as well. Participation in this market is also possible by acquisition of positions on the London Metal Exchange.

ZINC USES

By far, the galvanizing sector is the biggest and most important consumer of zinc and now accounts for about 45 percent of total demand. *Galvanizing*—the application of a protective coating on steel products—provides or enhances resistance to corrosion and rusting. The zinc coating may be applied by "hot dipping" (dipping the steel in a bath of molten zinc), electrogalvanizing (zinc plating), spraying, painting, or mechanical plating. Each

alloy: a mixture of two or more metals combined in order to attain certain physical characteristics such as hardness, color, resistance to rust, and corrosion, etc.

galvanizing: the application of a zinc coating to steel or other metals in order to prevent rusting and corrosion. Often the zinc coating is applied by dipping the steel in molten zinc or by electroplating.

technique offers different attributes—thickness, surface finish, degree of corrosion resistance, and cost—to the finished product.

The two most important uses of galvanized steel are the construction and auto industries. In the United States, these industries each consume about 40 percent of all galvanized steel shipments.

Outside the United States, the auto industry may account for only 20 percent and the construction industry as much as 60 percent of demand for galvanized steel products, but the fastest growing end-use sector is undoubtedly autos and other vehicles. Growth in the use of galvanized steel by the auto industry, which protects the frame and body from rusting and extends vehicle life, will reflect increasing hot-dip and electrogalvanizing capacity around the world and the trend toward quality among the auto manufacturers.

Construction is the largest end-use sector for galvanized products as well as for zinc overall. Among the particular uses for galvanized steel are structural beams, reinforcing rods, scaffolding, cladding and guttering, roofing, and window frames. In addition, brass is widely used by the building industry for plumbing and fixtures as well as door knobs and handles.

brass: an alloy containing usually 60% to 70% copper along with zinc and sometimes a trace amount of lead.

Zinc alloys, including *brass* and bronze, and die castings made with zinc and other metals, account for about 15 percent of total demand. The chemical industry is another important consumer, taking about 10 percent of total demand. Here, its major use is in zinc oxide, an essential ingredient in synthetic and natural rubber products. Automobile tires, for example, contain about 5 percent zinc oxide.

Because of its particular end uses, the demand for zinc is closely tied to business activity around the world.

As with many other metals and raw materials, a number of Asian and Latin American countries will fuel much of the growth in consumption during the 1990s. Usage trends—substitution to or away from zinc and the intensity of usage, particularly the thickness of coatings in galvanized steel products—will also have a bearing on the growth of overall demand during the years ahead.

Prospects for more infrastructure construction and repair in the United States as well as road and airport construction in Japan may be expected to impact demand for galvanized steel construction products in the years ahead.

The development of zinc-air batteries for use in personal computers is a promising new use that could become important in the middle to late 1990s. These batteries are said to last three times longer than the nickel-cadmium battery and are easily recycled.

ZINC SOURCES

Zinc, like lead, is mined in a number of countries around the world, and with the exception of Peru, primary output is located in regions not threatened by political and social factors. Australia and Canada are the two biggest producing countries and the United States is the fourth most important producer. However, labor disputes in Canada have in the past disrupted production with implications for the metal's price.

Table 5.1. Zinc Supply and Demand Balance (thousands of metric tons)

	1988	1989	1990	1991	1992
Mine production	5,052	5,092	5,390	5,500	5,662
Primary refined production	4,941	4,907	4,850	4,950	5,045
Secondary refined production	299	310	334	350	355
Total Refined Production	**5,240**	**5,217**	**5,184**	**5,300**	**5,400**
Net imports to East Bloc	−43	−42	39	40	45
Total Refined Supply	**5,197**	**5,175**	**5,223**	**5,340**	**5,445**
Total Refined Demand	**5,271**	**5,203**	**5,235**	**5,200**	**5,400**
Change in stocks	−74	−28	−12	140	45

As with many other metals markets, disruptions at any of the big producing mines—due to a labor strike or even a technical problem—can sometimes have sizable price implications. Indeed, labor disputes in Canada have in the past boosted the price of zinc in the world market.

Although not significant in the past, secondary supply sources of zinc are potentially important. With increased use of zinc-galvanized steel in the auto and construction industries, secondary zinc from electric arc furnaces is a growing source of recycled metal. In the past, these dusts were disposed of as hazardous industrial waste, but environmental concerns and increased disposal costs have provided an incentive to recycle these materials and new technologies are now making this possible.

Future market availability of zinc will also be affected by disposals from the U.S. strategic stockpile. The entire National Defense Stockpile of 344,000 tons is to be sold over five years.

Table 5.2.   Zinc Mine Production—Top Ten Producers (thousands of metric tons)

	1989	1990	1991	1992
Canada	1,216	1,203	1,148	1,314
Australia	811	884	1,048	1,025
Peru	598	584	623	600
United States	288	543	548	545
Mexico	284	307	317	325
Spain	266	257	265	202
Ireland	169	166	188	199
Sweden	163	158	157	170
Japan	132	127	133	132
Brazil	106	113	103	114

THE MARKET BALANCE

During the 1980s, annual deficits in most years resulted in a gradual decline in market stocks. This followed years of big deficits in the 1970s when poor business conditions for the auto and construction industries depressed consumption.

The 1990s began with surpluses once again as the global recession hit these two key industries for zinc. Prospects for the years ahead depend on the strength of auto sales and construction around the world. Assuming moderate growth around the world and increased demand, particularly in the newly industrialized countries, the zinc market could find itself in a deficit situation during the years ahead.

CHAPTER 6

Tin

Tin has been one of the least interesting metals to investors in recent years. In 1985, with the collapse of the International Tin Council's price support operations, prices fell sharply—and have languished ever since. The buildup in market stocks during the prior years of price support created an overhang that has been slowly worked off, reflecting the deficit of new supply relative to demand in most years since 1985.

Tin is accessible to investors through the London Metal Exchange or through a handful of publicly traded companies which produce the metal.

TIN USES

Solders recently replaced tinplate as the single largest end use for the metal, accounting for almost one-third of total tin consumption. Growing demand for tin-based solders reflects growth in the world electronics industry and increased production of TVs, VCRs, household appliances, and other electrical devices. Electronics accounts for over 50 percent of the tin used in solders.

solders: various alloys often containing lead or tin, used to join metals, such as electrical wiring or plumbing joints.

In many solders, tin is alloyed with lead, antimony, silver, or other metals. Metals such as indium and bismuth are added to tin-based solders to create fusible solders with lower melting points. A newly developed promising use for fusible solders is in the manufacture of plastic components with complex internal structures for use in the aerospace and auto industries. These plastic components are made using a fusible solder cast that can be melted away without damage to the cast plastic part.

Tinplate is the second most important application, accounting for about 30 percent of worldwide consumption of the metal. Tin-plated steel is used widely by the food and beverage industries for canning. Aluminum packaging is generally less expensive and has been taking marketshare from tin-plated steel except for large containers where aluminum may not offer sufficient rigidity. In addition, thinner tin coatings on food and beverage cans is reducing tin consumption per unit. Other substitutes—including non-tin-coated steel, chrome-plated steel, polymers, and plastics—are also competing with tin, reducing prospects for growth in tinplate use.

The fastest growing end-use sector for tin is in various chemical applications including plastic stabilizers, agricultural pesticides, antifouling paints for ships, and biocidal compounds used to protect paints, textiles, and building materials. Another relatively new use—in safe, nontoxic, easy-to-handle, tin-based fire retardants and smoke inhibitors—is promising.

Tin is also used in the manufacture of *pewterware*, in some *bronze* and brass and other tin-containing alloys. Many of these alloys are used in

pewterware: refers to kitchen and tabletop utensils, cookware, etc. fabricated from an alloy consisting chiefly of tin and also most frequently lead.

bronze: a copper-rich tin alloy that sometimes contains other elements such as zinc or phosphorus.

Table 6.1.   Tin Supply and Demand Balance (thousands of metric tons)

	1988	1989	1990	1991
Primary refined production	169	178	167	165
Secondary refined production	9	9	8	8
Government destocking	2	3	2	6
Total Refined Supply	**180**	**190**	**177**	**179**
Total Refined Demand	**179**	**179**	**180**	**181**
Net refined exports to East Bloc	13	9	0	0
Change in stocks	−12	2	−3	−2

construction, machinery, and consumer durables. In particular, tin-zinc alloys are known for their resistance to corrosion and tin-nickel alloys are used in coatings because of their hardness, lubricating qualities, and attractive appearance.

One of the most visible new uses of tin is in the sealants used to cover wine bottle tops. In the past, lead has dominated this market—but its use is declining because of its toxicity. Tin is an ideal substitute because it is nontoxic, attractive, and easily adapted to the existing capping technologies and equipment.

TIN SOURCES

World mine output of tin is concentrated in some six or seven countries. The top producers are Indonesia, Brazil, Malaysia, Bolivia, Thailand, China, and the former Soviet Union. For other metals, this concentration might give pause for concern—but not for tin, not at least in the current market environment of large aboveground inventories and ample excess capacity in many of the important producing companies. In future years, when aboveground stocks have been reduced to more normal levels and capacity utilization rates in the main producing countries have moved up sharply, mine supply disruptions might again be a factor to consider, but this is many years off.

Mine production in Brazil has fallen rapidly in recent years due to legal disputes over mining rights between corporate mining companies and independent prospectors, or garimpeiros, who are responsible for a significant share of Brazilian output. In addition, declining ore grades have hurt output.

The People's Republic of China has become an increasingly important mine producer of tin—and will likely expand production in the years ahead. Geologists say that the country's tin deposits are extensions of those found in other southeast Asian countries and according to the China National Nonferrous Metals Industry Corporation between 40 percent and 60 percent of mainland China's tin resources have not yet been exploited.

Malaysian tin production has fallen off sharply in recent years due to declining grades and high mining costs relative to the metal's price. Malaysia has, however, stepped up its imports of *concentrates* from other producing countries as feedstock for its tin smelters and remains one of the top producers of refined tin.

The United States is neither an important mine producer nor does it have significant tin *smelting* and refining capacity. However, the U.S. Defense Logistics Agency has maintained strategic stockpiles of tin. In fiscal 1992, almost 8,700 tons of tin were sold by the U.S. government and 12,000 tons

concentrates: semi-processed mine ore that has already had some of the impurities or unwanted minerals removed but which needs further upgrading through smelting and/or refining

smelting: the process of extracting crude metal from ore or concentrate prior to actual refining..

Table 6.2. Tin Mine Production in Concentrates Top Producers (metric tons)

	1989	1990	1991
China	33,000	35,800	33,700
Indonesia	31,600	30,200	30,100
Brazil	50,200	39,100	29,300
Malaysia	32,000	28,500	20,700
Bolivia	15,800	17,300	16,800
Former Soviet Union	14,000	13,000	11,000
Thailand	14,700	14,600	10,900
Peru	5,100	5,100	6,600
Australia	7,800	7,400	5,700
All others	19,300	18,200	14,400
Total	**223,500**	**209,200**	**179,200**

were authorized for sale in fiscal 1993 (which began on October 1, 1992). Continued sales of these magnitudes are likely during the next few years.

THE MARKET BALANCE

Although the tin market is likely to remain in a small net deficit position during the middle and late 1990s, the level of inventories overhanging the market will remain large and prices will probably continue to trade in a fairly narrow range. For the next few years, at least, most metals analysts believe that tin will likely remain one of the least exciting investment metals.

CHAPTER 7

Aluminum

A luminum is the most abundant metal in the earth's crust. But, unlike most other metals, aluminum is never found in its pure native state. Instead, the metal most often exists as an oxide (in chemical combinations with the element oxygen), usually with other chemicals and impurities. The most common form of aluminum ore is *bauxite*. Bauxite ore is the principal raw material feedstock for aluminum smelters.

In its pure refined form, aluminum is a bluish silver-white color. However, a thin coating of oxygen forms when the metal is exposed to air, resulting in a dullish luster that most of us are familiar with from the various aluminum products we come in contact with in our daily lives. It is this oxygen coating that imparts a high resistance to corrosion, making aluminum especially useful in a number of applications from food packaging to home siding to auto bodies. Its other characteristics—high conductivity of both electricity and heat, malleability, ductility, light reflectivity, and heat radiation—make it useful in a wide range of applications. Alloying aluminum with other metals (such as copper, magnesium, silicon, or zinc, for example) enhances its characteristics,

bauxite: hydrated aluminum oxide $(Al_2O_3 \cdot 2H_2O)$, the principal ore from which aluminum is extracted.

especially its tensile strength, hardness, and corrosive resistance, and increases its versatility.

Aluminum equities are generally the most popular vehicle for investors and there are a number of major aluminum companies the shares of which trade on major U.S. and Canadian exchanges. Aluminum futures contracts also trade on the Commodity Exchange Inc. (COMEX), but trading is usually not very active. The London Metal Exchange also trades aluminum.

ALUMINUM USES

In its pure form and in alloys, aluminum is one of the most widely used metals. Transportation equipment (autos, trains, aircraft) accounts for about one-quarter of total consumption. Building materials and packaging each take another 20 percent or so of annual supply. Other major end-use sectors are electrical, machinery and equipment, and consumer durables.

In the transportation sector, aluminum has been used increasingly in the past two decades as a substitute for steel, largely to reduce the weight of vehicles and help the manufacturers meet government fuel efficiency and pollution emission restrictions. The typical U.S. automobile now uses about 200 pounds of the metal while Japanese cars typically contain about 225 pounds, although there is much variation from one manufacturer and car model to the next. On the plus side, automakers are researching new applications for the metal, particularly in aluminum-based alloys and composites.

Elsewhere in the transportation industry, the metal's combination of light weight and strength make it attractive for use in aircraft, train and subway cars, and ships. On the negative side, the metal faces stiff competition in the aircraft industry from composites (especially carbon-fiber composites), ceramics, polymers, and other specialty metals such as titanium. Aluminum producers, however, are working to develop aluminum-based composites that will compete with these lighter, stronger substitutes.

In the construction and building sector, aluminum is used for siding; roofing; window, door, and building frames; screens; and a variety of other applications. Competition is also a threat to some of these uses. For example, vinyl is replacing aluminum in the residential siding, wood is staging a comeback in framing, and nylon is now used in some screens.

The fastest growing use of aluminum, in addition to the transportation sector, is packaging—aluminum foil, flexible packaging, and food and beverage containers. The modern "tin" can contains no tin but is rolled aluminum. In the United States, 95 percent of all beverage cans are made from aluminum. Consumers favor aluminum packaging because it is lightweight, convenient, recyclable, and hygienic.

In addition to the potential for aluminum alloys and composites, another promising new use is the aluminum air-cell battery developed by Alcan. Because of its long shelflife, low weight, and constant power output, the air-cell battery is especially well suited for a number of possible applications including electric vehicles.

ALUMINUM SOURCES

Bauxite ores are the principal source of primary aluminum. Bauxite is mined in a large number of

Table 7.1. Aluminum Supply and Demand Balance (thousands of metric tons)

	1988	1989	1990	1991	1992	1993
Mine production	6,721	7,139	7,213	7,396	7,370	7,500
Scrap and other refined production	1,253	1,194	1,252	1,129	1,465	1,515
Total Refined Production	**7,974**	**8,333**	**8,465**	**8,525**	**8,835**	**9,015**
East Bloc exports	248	233	320	351	575	525
Total Refined Supply	**8,182**	**8,566**	**8,785**	**8,876**	**9,410**	**9,540**
Total refined consumption	8,190	8,637	8,761	8,969	9,030	9,020
East Block imports	97	86	67	39	250	300
Total Refined Demand	**8,287**	**8,763**	**8,828**	**9,008**	**9,280**	**9,320**
Change in stocks	−105	−197	−43	−132	130	220

countries around the world, with no one or two countries accounting for a dominant share of global output. The three biggest producers are Guinea (in Africa) with 17 million metric tons, Jamaica with 12 million tons, and Brazil with about 10 million tons of annual bauxite production. The United States mines only 50,000 tons while the former Soviet Union mines about 5 million tons a year. Aggregate annual world production of bauxite is about 100 million tons per year excluding the former Soviet Union and East Bloc and about 110 million tons including this group of countries.

alumina: an oxide of aluminum often produced from bauxite ore as the first step in manufacturing aluminum.

Bauxite is converted to *alumina,* an intermediate product, and finally aluminum through smelting, a chemical reduction process requiring huge amounts of electricity. But the major aluminum smelters and aluminum fabricating companies are often based in countries other than the sources of bauxite. For example, the United States which is not a significant bauxite mining country is the world's biggest primary producer of aluminum with annual output of more than 4 million metric tons. The former Soviet Union produces some 2 million to 2.5 million tons per annum and Canada is the third most important producer with almost 2 million tons. Total primary production of aluminum runs about 18 million tons per year including the former Soviet Union and East Bloc. Excluding these countries, world production is 14 million to 15 million tons.

In recent years, a heavy flow of metal from the former Soviet Union has contributed to aluminum price weakness. Estimated exports have risen from under 300,000 tons in 1990 to some 1.2 million tons annually in 1992 to 1993, roughly equal to 8 percent of western world output. Many analysts believe that this heavy flow of aluminum into world markets could continue for a few more years.

In addition to mine production, old scrap—principally from recycled beverage cans and junked autos—contributes a significant quantity of metal to the market each year. Secondary supply of aluminum is increasing around the world reflecting increased recycling and improvements in scrap collection systems. By 1992 to 1993, secondary supply was probably running around 6 million metric tons per year. In the United States, about 60 billion aluminum cans are recycled annually.

As noted above, aluminum smelters consume tremendous amounts of energy, but *refining* of scrap requires less than 5 percent of the energy used to make the original metal. As a result, energy represents only about 2 percent of a secondary aluminum smelter but over 25 percent of a primary smelter.

refining: the metallurgical process of upgrading and purifying minerals, metals, and industrial scrap into high-grade metal meeting acceptable industrial standards.

The most significant national producers of aluminum from recycled scrap are the United States with 2.1 million tons, Japan with 1.5 million tons, and Germany with roughly half a million metric tons. In the United States, more than 40 percent of aluminum fabrication demand was satisfied by secondary supplies.

In Table 7.1, the component of supply arising from recycling is often designated "refined secondary production." Total refined production, that is all of the aluminum which is available to the market, is the sum of refined mine production plus refined secondary production plus East Bloc exports into the world market.

THE MARKET BALANCE

The aluminum market has been in surplus during the early 1990s with total supplies exceeding consumption resulting in a buildup of visible inventories. As a result of this market surplus, the price of aluminum was under pressure falling from a peak of $1.65 per pound in 1988 to 55 cents to 60 cents per pound in 1991 to 1993.

The shift from deficit in the middle 1980s to a big surplus in recent years reflected poor economic circumstances in the major aluminum-consuming markets and consequently slower growth in demand versus steady production and surging shipments from the former Soviet Union. While U.S. producers have cut back, reflecting lower prices (and in 1993 due to weather-related electric power shortages in the Pacific Northwest), output has continued to rise in Canada, Europe, and the Middle East.

Many analysts expect improving fortunes for aluminum in the mid-1990s as business conditions and aluminum consumption improve and Russian shipments taper off. Meanwhile, reflecting the past period of lower prices, additions to production capacity are likely to slow. Although still uncertain, the Clinton administration's proposed energy taxes could jeopardize some U.S. aluminum capacity, cutting the country's aluminum output, possibly benefitting the world market price, but nevertheless hurting the American aluminum companies.

CHAPTER 8

Nickel

I ron ore, steel, chrome, cobalt, manganese, molyb-
denum, tungsten, and nickel are among the so-
called steel industry metals. In addition to iron ore
(the chief constituent of steel) and steel itself, these
others are used extensively in various steel alloys.
Of these, nickel is the most interesting to investors—because it is accessible through established nickel mining companies and because it is
often an exciting market that can be played by the
more aggressive investor/speculator on the London
Metal Exchange.

Nickel's physical properties—especially its corrosion resistance and high strength even at elevated
temperatures, its attractive appearance, and its ability to lend these characteristics to nickel-containing alloys—makes the metal useful in a broad range
of industry applications.

Stainless steel production is the major end use for
nickel, accounting for approximately 66 percent of
average annual demand. In addition to stainless,
nickel is used in other alloy steels and nonferrous
nickel-based alloys, electroplating, foundry products,
and copper-based alloys. In turn, stainless steel and
other nickel products are used in a very wide range

stainless steel:
alloy principally
of steel and also
frequently nickel
which imparts a
high resistance
to rusting and
corrosion.

electroplating:
the process by
which a very fine
coat of one metal,
such as nickel,
gold, or silver, is
deposited on
another metal by
passing an electric
current through a
liquid solution be-
tween a cathode
and an anode
made of each
metal, respectively.

of industries and applications, so that both stainless steel demand and nickel demand is dictated by the trends in economic activity in the major countries.

While nickel consumption is concentrated in the major industrial nations, mine supplies are to a large extent dominated by the former Soviet Union, especially Russia. The former Soviet Union accounts for nearly one-third of total annual mine supply so that economic and political trends in these republics are particularly important to the nickel market and the metal's price prospects.

Canada is the next largest producer with output of about 190,000 to 200,000 metric tons per annum. New Caledonia and Australia follow with yearly production of roughly 100,000 tons and 65,000 to 70,000 tons, respectively. The United States produced no nickel prior to 1990, but in recent years has had a trickle of output. In 1992, U.S. nickel mine production was close to 5,000 tons.

Nickel mining equities are generally the most popular vehicle for investors although there are only three major companies—Inco, Falconbridge (a subsidiary of Noranda), and Cominco. All three trade on major U.S. and Canadian exchanges. Nickel futures contracts and options also trade on the London Metal Exchange.

NICKEL USES

As noted, nickel's chief use is in the production of stainless steel and a variety of other alloys and products. In all, the metal is used as an alloying agent in more than 3,000 different alloys that are used in more than a quarter-million specific end-use applications. As an example, nickel is important in the chemical and food-processing industries where its resistance to corrosion make it an important element in the manufacturing of equipment and machinery. It is used in nuclear power plants and aerospace equipment because it not only resists corrosion but is unaffected by extremely high temperatures. In addition, the metal is used in oil and gas pipelines, electrical equipment, batteries, catalysts, and many more applications.

Nickel-containing stainless steel tanks are used for road, rail, and naval transport of various liquids ranging from dairy products, petrochemicals, and toxic chemicals and wastes. In addition, to corrosion resistance and strength, the ease of cleaning makes the metal especially suitable for this type of use.

The auto industry in recent years has also begun to use zinc-nickel coated steel for certain body panels and structural parts. These coatings provide significantly more resistance to corrosion from road salt than ordinary galvanized steel.

Metal analysts anticipate that nickel stainless steel, new high-performance alloys, and electroplating will be important growth areas for the metal. The electronics industry is also expected to use more nickel in future years.

NICKEL SOURCES

Russia is the world's largest producer of nickel with estimated annual mine output of 180,000 to 200,000 metric tons. Russian exports to the West increased sharply in the early 1990s as authorities sold metal from above ground stocks in order to raise desperately needed foreign exchange. Falling internal consumption of nickel in the early 1990s also led some

Table 8.1.   Nickel Supply and Demand Balance (thousands of metric tons)

	1989	1990	1991	1992	1993
Total refined production	573	571	596	580	550
East Bloc exports	100	100	125	110	100
Total Refined Supply	**673**	**671**	**721**	**690**	**650**
Total Refined Consumption (excluding the use of scrap supplies)	**620**	**685**	**678**	**620**	**625**
Change in stocks	53	−14	43	70	25

industrial users to transform primary nickel into high-grade scrap for export, thereby bypassing official export controls to the West.

At the same time, actual mine output fell sharply due to various problems at the Noril'sk metal mining complex in Siberia, the principal nickel producer. Mining, like other aspects of the Russian economy, has suffered from a lack of capital investment, poor maintenance, fuel shortages, labor problems, and other difficulties. In addition, Russia's nickel refining capacity has also suffered from the same set of problems.

Although little is known outside Russia about the level of inventories and the actual rates of nickel mine production, most observers believe that the rate of nickel sales by the former Soviet Union must fall off sharply in the middle 1990s as stocks are depleted. Meanwhile, the prospective level of nickel production in the next few years is especially difficult to predict. On the one hand, the mining industry has been neglected for many years. But, a few western mining companies have begun to make major investments in Russia that will eventually boost mine output and world supplies of nickel.

For example, the large Finnish company, Out-okumpu Mining, has established a joint venture to mine nickel and modernize the Pechenga nickel smelter on the Kola Peninsula. This could begin to affect production by 1995–1996. Meanwhile, Inco has entered into various agreements to transfer mining, smelting, and refining technology to the Noril'sk nickel mining complex.

Canada is the second largest national producer of nickel with annual output of roughly 190,000 to 200,000 metric tons. Reflecting the weakness in the nickel price itself, the major Canadian producers also cut back on annual output and capital investment during the early 1990s. Australia is a distant third with nickel mine production near 65,000 to 70,000 tons per year.

THE MARKET BALANCE

Reduced demand and increased shipments from the former Soviet Union have resulted in a sizable market surplus during the early 1990s. The counterpart to this surplus has been rising inventory levels at London Metal Exchange warehouses, refiners, and mining companies. Not surprisingly, nickel prices were depressed in the early 1990s.

Until prices begin to recover, Canadian mine production is likely to be restrained by the major producing companies. Russian nickel output is under pressure too, for some of the reasons just discussed, but until above ground inventories are fairly well depleted export levels could remain high in relationship to world market conditions.

At some point in the middle 1990s, improving economic activity in the industrial nations should be reflected in rising consumption of stainless steel and other nickel applications. In tandem with lower Russian exports, world nickel prices must also begin to recover offering attractive opportunities to metals investors.

PART 3

PRECIOUS METALS

CHAPTER 9

Gold

O f all metals, gold is the most familiar to investors because more than any other metal it is a monetary asset and investment medium in its own right. Indeed, mankind has valued gold as a store of value, medium of exchange, and unit of account for millennia. Today, gold remains one of the most liquid, well-known, and widely accepted investments.

Gold investors have the widest choice of vehicles including *bullion* bars and coins; bullion proxies, such as storage accounts and certificates; mining equities; futures; and options on both futures and mining stocks. This range offers opportunities to both the risk-averse investor and the risk-oriented speculator. And gold's special properties make it attractive to many investors as a portfolio diversifier, as a hedge against inflation and currency instability, and as insurance against stock market and other risks.

bullion: fine gold or silver usually in bars or ingots generally refined to a purity of at least 99%. This is the form in which central banks and investors hold gold and which is the raw material for industrial users and jewelry manufacturers.

ingot: a bar of gold, silver, or another metal.

GOLD USES

Today, the single largest consumer of gold is the jewelry industry. In fact, demand for gold by jewelry

61

fabricators in recent years has exceeded annual mine production in the West, excluding the former Soviet Union and East Bloc countries. In recent years, jewelry fabrication has literally grown by leaps and bounds and, by the early 1990s, consumed roughly 65 million to 80 million ounces per annum.

To be fair, however, it is important to understand that jewelry is purchased by many people around the world, especially in the Middle East and Asia, as a savings and investment medium rather than as a luxury good and personal adornment. In these countries, jewelry tends to be of higher purity, usually 21 to 24 *karats*—88 percent to 100 percent pure. It also tends to sell at a much lower mark-up over the value of its gold content, sometimes by as little as 10 percent to 20 percent. In these countries, demand is responsive to the price of gold itself. Lower prices typically generate increased demand for jewelry as a vehicle for savings and investment. In addition, demand is usually related to the state of the domestic economy and the amount of personal income available for saving.

In contrast, in the industrial nations—here in the United States as well as in Western Europe, and Japan—jewelry is purchased principally as a luxury good and fashion item for adornment. In these countries, the purity of the gold used for jewelry fabrication is also much lower, ranging from 8 karat (which is only 33 percent pure) to 18 karat (which is 75 percent fine gold). Ironically, the retail price of jewelry in these countries carries a huge mark-up over the cost of the gold itself, often as much as 200 percent to 400 percent.

karat: a measure of the purity of precious metals based on a system of 24. Totally pure gold, for example, is 24 karat. 14 karat gold, which is the norm for jewelry in the United States, is 14 parts pure gold and 10 parts other metals.

Since the late 1980s, worldwide jewelry demand for gold has grown by leaps and bounds from about 38 million ounces in 1986 to around 80 million ounces in 1993 despite the slowdown in economic growth in many countries. Gold experts expect strong growth in global jewelry demand to continue during the middle to late 1990s.

A number of factors have contributed to this rapid growth in jewelry demand. First, to jewelry manufacturers and consumers in many countries around the world, gold is cheap when denominated in local currencies and particularly when adjusted for inflation over the past 10 to 15 years. Second, demographic trends in many countries are supportive with more people moving into those age groups with a high propensity to buy gold jewelry and with the increasing economic independence of women contributing toward their direct purchases. And, third, rising prosperity in countries like China and India where jewelry is savings-related and is used as a means to accumulate wealth.

In addition to jewelry, as can be seen from Table 9.1, about 8.5 million to 9 million ounces of gold are used each year in a variety of other industrial uses. The two biggest nonjewelry uses of gold are in electronics and dentistry. Unlike jewelry usage, the aggregate of other industrial uses of gold will probably not change enough from one year to the next to have much influence on the market's fundamentals and the metal's price prospects.

Gold's high electrical conductivity, its resistance to corrosion even at high temperatures, its ductility and workability have assured that no other metal can substitute for gold as a contact and

Table 9.1.   Gold Supply and Demand Balance (millions of ounces)

	1987	1988	1989	1990	1991	1992[a]	1993[a]
Mine production							
South Africa	19.5	20.0	19.6	19.4	19.2	19.6	19.2
United States	5.0	6.5	8.3	9.3	9.6	10.3	10.6
Canada	3.7	4.3	5.1	5.3	5.6	5.1	5.0
Australia	3.6	5.0	6.2	7.8	7.6	7.6	7.2
Brazil	2.7	3.2	3.1	2.7	2.1	1.8	1.6
Other market economies	10.0	10.8	10.9	12.0	12.9	14.0	15.0
Total	**44.5**	**49.8**	**53.2**	**56.5**	**57.0**	**58.4**	**58.6**
Forward sales/gold loans	3.5	15.0	10.0	5.5	6.0	9.0	5.0
Other short sales	0.0	0.0	0.0	3.0	5.0	10.0	0.0
Old scrap	11.0	10.0	9.0	10.5	8.5	7.5	7.0
East Bloc sales							
Russia and other CIS[b]	4.6	3.2	7.8	14.1	15.9	12.0	4.0
China	2.8	2.9	2.9	3.0	3.0	2.5	2.5
North Korea	0.5	0.6	0.6	0.6	0.6	0.5	0.5
Total	**7.9**	**6.7**	**11.3**	**17.7**	**19.5**	**15.0**	**7.0**
Total Supply	**66.9**	**81.5**	**83.5**	**93.2**	**96.0**	**99.9**	**77.6**
Jewelry	39.1	49.3	61.3	65.5	67.9	76.0	80.5
Industrial use	7.4	7.8	8.1	8.5	8.6	8.7	8.9
Total Fabrication	**46.5**	**57.1**	**69.4**	**74.0**	**76.5**	**84.7**	**89.4**
Total Stock Changes	**20.4**	**24.4**	**14.1**	**19.2**	**19.5**	**15.2**	**−11.8**
of which:							
Official purchase or sales(−)[c]	2.5	7.0	−5.0	0.0	−5.0	−20.9	−6.0
Net private investment—Total	17.9	17.4	19.1	19.2	24.5	36.1	−5.8
Coinage[d]	7.0	4.7	4.7	4.9	5.6	4.0	6.0
Bullion surplus	10.9	12.7	14.4	14.3	18.9	32.1	−11.8

[a] APMA estimates for 1992 and projections 1993.
[b] Russia and other CIS Sales include net central bank transactions by these countries.
[c] Includes forward sales by the Netherlands in 1992. Excludes official transactions by Russia and other CIS republics.
[d] Coinage includes bullion, commemorative, and imitation coins as well as medals and medallions.
Copyright 1993—American Precious Metals Advisors, Inc.

conductor in everything from household appliances to space satellites and rockets. In recent years, the worldwide use of gold by the electrical and elec-tronics industry has amounted to just over 4.5 mil-lion ounces per year.

In dentistry, gold's resistance to corrosion, its *malleability*, and nontoxicity make it ideal for crowns, bridges, and fillings either on its own or as an alloy with other metals. Dental use of gold now totals about 1.6 million ounces each year.

GOLD SOURCES

Although gold mining occurs around the world, the bulk of current mine output is concentrated in only a few countries. Approximately one-third of total mine output (excluding the former Soviet Union and other East Bloc countries) is from South Africa. Remarkably, gold mine output in this country has held steady around 19.5 million to 20 million ounces per year during the late 1980s and early 1990s despite the erosion in profitability, the decline in ore grades, and the political-related difficulties facing the South African mining industry.

Some analysts believe that the political changes in South Africa will trigger a new wave of invest-ment in the country's mining industry. If so, gold production could begin rising again later in the decade.

The United States has become the second most important gold mining country in recent years with production rising above 10 million ounces annually. Following years of rapid expansion, reflecting the development of a few big deposits, growth in gold output is already slowing and total output could

malleability: the ability of a metal to be shaped with-out breaking, cracking, or rup-ture. Gold is the most malleable of all metals, a char-acteristic which makes the yellow metal exception-ally workable by jewelry fabricators and dentists.

Total output from US could begin to decline later in the decade.

begin to decline later in the decade. Among the factors contributing to the expected downturn in U.S. gold mine output are the growing costs of meeting government environmental regulations and the increased federal royalties imposed on mine revenues. Canada's gold mine output, about half that of the United States, is already falling because of the rising environmental costs and less favorable tax treatment of the industry for exploration and development compared to the 1980s.

Russia and the People's Republic of China are also important gold mining countries. Russian production has fallen from around 8 million to 9 million ounces per year in the late 1980s to roughly 6 million ounces per year in the mid-1990s. This decline was symptomatic of the problems affecting all areas of the Russian economy—and prospects are very much geared to the overall performance of Russian industry in the years ahead. China mined about 3.5 million to 4 million ounces per year in the early 1990s, roughly double the country's output in the early 1980s. And, in contrast to the trend in almost every other major gold mining country, the gradual expansion in China's output should continue.

In addition to current output, the mining industry contributes to current market supply through its *forward sales* and price *hedging* activities. Through a complicated series of hedge-related and/or arbitrage transactions by bullion dealers, the forward sales of mining companies result in an immediate increase in available supply even though the actual gold sold may not yet have been mined by the company. As can be seen by the table on gold supply and demand, this has been an important component of supply since the late 1980s.

forward sales: an agreement similar to a futures contract for the sale of a commodity on a specified future date at a preset price. Mining companies may sell forward in order to "lock in" or hedge the price they will receive when they deliver their metal production to the buyer.

hedging: the reduction of price risk by miners or industrial users of metals, often through the forward sale or purchase of the metal to "lock in" its price prior to the time of actual delivery or through the purchase of call or put options.

"the forward sales of mining co's result in an immediate increase in available supply even though the actual gold sold may not yet been mined by the company."

are:

1. Expectations about the ... ce itself. If mine executives expect a rising price trend, they are less apt to sell forward or otherwise hedge their price risk—but if they expect falling prices, they will hedge aggressively, adding to current supply.
2. The trend in actual mine output. If output is falling, there are fewer ounces to sell forward.
3. The price miners can receive for their forward sales. To a large extent, this is a function of interest rates. Falling interest rates decrease the price received on forward sales and vice versa.

INTEREST RATES (FUNCTION)

As with other metals, the recycling of old scrap—from discarded electronics and telecommunications equipment, from old jewelry, from dental waste, and from other gold-bearing items—contributes a significant quantity of metal to the market each year. The quantity of old scrap each year is most of all related to the price of gold. During the 1980s and early 1990s, the amount of gold coming from old scrap has generally trended downward reflecting the downtrend in the price of gold. And, in the future, scrap supply will probably continue to reflect the trend in the metal's price.

Price of scraps gld goes down when price of gold goes down.

THE MARKET BALANCE

From time immemorial, the gold market has been a market in surplus. Year in and year out, current supply has always exceeded jewelry and other fabrication demand—and there has been a surplus available to satisfy investment and central bank demand. This surplus has been definitionally equivalent to the total change in market stocks each year.

In turn, the change in stocks has several components: official (central bank) purchases or sales, gold coinage, and bullion bar hoarding (the bullion surplus). In 1991–1992, however, the official sector was a big seller of gold from central bank reserves. This was a major bearish factor during those years and required investors around the world to buy a huge quantity of bullion bars, something they were willing to do only at much lower price levels.

"In 1991–1992 ... the official sector was a big seller of gold from central bank reserves. This was a major bearish factor during those years and required investors around the world to buy a huge quantity of bullion bars, something they were willing to do only at much lower price levels".

Silver

S ilver, or poor man's gold as it was once known, has become principally an industrial metal in recent years, reflecting the gradual loss of its monetary/financial characteristics and its diminishing appeal to investors. Although still considered a precious metal, its price has fallen to roughly one-eightieth that of gold versus one-twentieth a couple of decades earlier.

As with gold, silver offers a wide variety of investment vehicles from which to choose—bullion bars and coins, *storage accounts* and *certificates*, mining equities, futures, and options on both futures and mining stocks. Although many investors at one time owned silver as a hedge asset—for insurance against inflation, currency depreciation, stock market risk, and so on—its poor price performance and changed market fundamentals mean that silver can no longer be relied upon to fulfill a hedge function.

storage accounts: precious metals investment programs offered by some brokerage firms and banks which allow investors to own metal without the inconvenience of taking delivery or personal storage.

SILVER USES

Testimony to silver's industrial nature is the fact that its single largest end use, by far, is for photographic films and papers. Silver nitrate crystals are

Photographic uses.

certificates: a convenient vehicle for metals investors attesting to ownership of a specific quantity of the underlying metal that is held on behalf of the owner by a bank, brokerage house, or bullion dealer in a recognized depository or warehouse. Most often used by precious metals investors, certificates allow investors to avoid the costs of delivery and, where applicable, sales taxes.

sterling: silver of a standard purity consisting of 925 parts fine silver and 75 parts copper. Sterling is the typical purity of silver tableware, household items, and jewelry.

the light-sensitive agent that makes the recording of images possible. As can be seen from Table 10.1, the photographic industry now consumes about 215 million ounces of silver each year, accounting for roughly 36 percent of total fabrication demand.

One of the most serious threats to the silver price is the development of silverless photography utilizing electronic photo imaging. Already, in the past decade, for example, the advent of the VCR and the camcorder has relegated 8 millimeter home movie film to the dustbin of history. Similar electronic imaging technology now threatens silver usage for still photography. To date, consumers and most professional photographers find the new technology too expensive, too inconvenient, and of inadequate quality in terms of print resolution.

In contrast, some silver bulls believe that the growth in conventional photography throughout the newly industrialized and developing world—particularly in big population countries like China and India—will be the more important trend in future years, contributing to a steady rise in silver demand from this sector. Certainly, if you are considering silver-related investments, you must carefully analyze the prospects for silver usage by the world photo industry over the time horizon relevant to your investment.

After photography, the next most important use of silver is in jewelry, *sterling* silverware and other household or decorative items. Silver consumption by this sector totals 130 million to 140 million ounces per year. Demand trends here are dependent on fashion, demographics, and price. After the silver price explosion in the late 1970s through 1980, consumers cut back on their purchases of these items.

Silver

0.1.   Silver Supply and Demand Balance (millions of ounces)

	1987	1988	1989	1990	1991	1992[a]	1993[a]
...duction							
	69.8	70.0	70.0	67.9	62.7	64.0	64.3
	39.8	53.4	60.8	66.5	61.0	61.0	63.4
	63.6	47.7	56.8	55.5	56.9	51.0	47.0
	38.1	44.1	41.3	44.4	40.9	41.5	43.0
	35.9	35.8	37.3	37.8	38.0	37.5	37.3
	16.1	16.3	17.7	20.4	29.7	31.5	32.0
...omies	71.4	73.0	71.6	74.5	75.9	82.5	83.5
Total Mine Production	**334.6**	**340.2**	**355.5**	**367.0**	**365.2**	**369.0**	**370.5**
Secondary supply							
Old scrap—Photographic	111.3	128.4	130.4	138.9	141.0	142.8	144.6
Old scrap—Other	60.0	70.0	75.0	65.0	60.0	50.0	50.0
Coin melt	14.0	13.0	10.0	8.0	6.0	5.0	4.0
Total Secondary Supply[b]	**185.3**	**211.4**	**215.4**	**211.9**	**207.0**	**197.8**	**198.6**
Indian domestic recycling	14.5	13.2	1.9	1.0	11.0	4.0	6.0
South Asian imports (−)	−4.7	−9.3	−29.5	−67.7	−47.2	−37.0	−55.0
Government disposals	20.0	8.0	11.0	11.0	12.0	10.0	12.0
Total Supply	**549.7**	**563.5**	**554.3**	**523.2**	**548.0**	**543.8**	**532.1**
Net CIS/East Bloc trade	6.0	−16.0	−10.0	−5.0	0.0	−5.0	−10.0
Fabrication demand[b]							
Photography	173.9	188.8	191.7	204.3	207.4	210.0	215.3
Jewelry, silverware, etc.	100.5	104.9	114.7	128.8	132.8	134.9	140.3
Electronics	87.3	92.9	100.4	104.9	95.0	94.6	95.0
Other industrial	90.8	91.7	98.9	108.2	111.6	112.1	112.7
Coinage	30.4	25.3	26.3	29.8	29.9	30.0	30.0
Total Fabrication	**482.9**	**503.6**	**532.0**	**576.0**	**576.7**	**581.6**	**593.3**
Net Private Investment[b]	**72.8**	**43.9**	**12.3**	**−57.8**	**−28.7**	**−42.8**	**−71.2**

[a] APMA projections for 1992 and 1993.
[b] Excludes CIS, East Bloc and South Asia. Totals may not add due to rounding.

Source: American Precious Metals Advisors. Copyright 1993—American Precious Metals Advisors, Inc.

At the same time, newly married couples in many of the industrial countries were less interested in acquiring sterling tableware, reflecting changing fashions and life-styles. In more recent years, lower prices, demographic trends, and the rising popularity of low-priced silver jewelry has fostered a recovery in usage by this sector.

Silver use in electronics—in conductors, contacts, and solders—is the third most important use consuming 90 million to 100 million ounces per year. One would think with the explosion in consumer demand for electronics goods and household appliances that silver use by this industry would be rising rapidly. However, offsetting the rise in the number of units sold—of TVs, radios, refrigerators, and so on—has been the opposing trend of miniaturization of silver-containing parts and economization in silver applications.

SILVER SOURCES

Excluding the former Soviet Union, Eastern Europe, and East Bloc countries, world silver mine production totaled about 370 million ounces per year in the early 1990s. The vast majority of this output is a *byproduct* or *coproduct* of *base metal* and gold mines. Various estimates suggest that from 70 percent to 85 percent of world silver mine output in the early 1990s was a byproduct or coproduct of other metal mining activities. As a result, the link between trends in silver mine supply and price is a tenuous one. Instead, mine production of silver in the market economy nations is more dependent on: (1) market conditions and production trends for other metals, including copper, lead, zinc, and gold; and

byproduct: a secondary metal that is produced in the mining of another metal and the value of which in terms of revenue generation is not of great importance to the economics of the mine.

coproducts: metals that are mined together, both of which are valuable contributors to overall mine revenue.

base metal: any of a number of non-precious metals that lose their metallic luster and readily tarnish at normal temperatures. Examples include iron, copper, lead, zinc, and nickel.

(2) country specific developments in the major silver mining nations.

Mexico is the largest producer with annual output close to 64 million ounces. Silver output has actually declined in the past few years from a record 70 million ounces in both 1988 and 1989. But, local observers believe that output will begin to improve in the next few years thanks to (1) an improved political and economic situation which together have enhanced the country's attractiveness to both foreign and domestic investors, (2) privatization of the mining industry, and (3) the easing of regulations relating to both the mining industry and foreign investment.

The United States has become the world's second biggest silver mining nation in recent years with annual output nearly as great as that of Mexico. Rapid expansion of output in the late 1980s reflected both the development of several new mines with very significant byproduct contributions and to the collapse in Peru's mining industry, which had previously held the second-place position. Most industry analysts believe that the growth in future silver mine production will be much more moderate, reflecting a slowdown in the development of new base metal and gold mines in the United States.

During the late 1980s and early 1990s, silver mine production in Peru has been hit hard by the country's political, social, labor, and economic problems as well as by the reign of terror imposed by the Maoist Shining Path. The deteriorating economic situation, shortages of mining supplies and equipment, and even the lack of cash to pay mine workers has put a terrific strain on the mining industry. Output has fallen from 63.6 million ounces in 1987 to probably around 51 million ounces this year.

Canada is the fourth biggest national producer of silver. Only about 25 percent to 30 percent of the country's silver output is main product. The bulk of production is associated with copper and lead/zinc mines. Following a pattern not too different from the U.S. silver industry, Canada's mine output fell from 44.4 million ounces in 1990 to under 41 million ounces in 1991 as reserves at the large Equity silver mine fell and as byproduct output eased with the decline in lead and zinc production.

As with other metals, secondary supply or the recycling of old scrap—from spent photographic films, papers, and developing solutions, as well as from discarded electronics and telecommunications equipment, from old jewelry, silverware, and other household items, and from other silver-bearing items—contributes a significant quantity of metal to the market each year. In addition, there has been a regular flow of supply from the recycling of old silver coins which have been dishoarded by investors and coin collectors. Secondary supply has contributed roughly 200 million ounces a year to the market during the early 1990s.

In the silver market, the quantity of scrap each year is related to the past usage of photographic materials (from which silver is recovered) in the prior couple of years, the scrapage rate of other old electronics equipment, and to the metal's price itself. In recent years, as can be seen from the supply/demand table, silver scrap supply has edged lower. While photographic scrap has continued to grow, reflecting the growth in picture taking around the world, other scrap and coin melt—both of which are extremely price responsive—have followed the price down.

In addition to mine production and secondary supply, silver sales from government stockpiles have regularly contributed metal to the market for many years. However, not since the early 1970s have government silver sales from monetary reserves or strategic stockpiles been a significant factor greatly affecting the metal's price.

The United States and several other governments still have significant holdings which remain from the days of silver coinage, or in official monetary reserves and in strategic defense stockpiles. Now, however, prospective government sales appear likely to be limited to quantities sufficient to supply the various *commemorative* and *bullion coin* programs that have become popular in many countries. But metals investors must be attuned to the possibility that large government silver disposals might be a price depressant in the future.

Other Supply/Demand Factors

Although India and the rest of the Indian subcontinent have little domestic silver mine production, the metal has for centuries been an integral part of the region's economic, political, and social landscape. Indeed, it is in this region alone where investment interest in silver remains robust. Today, the subcontinent retains private silver holdings on the order of 4.7 billion ounces. Of this, possibly 80 percent—about 3.8 billion ounces—is in India itself.

Changes in hoarding demand have led to substantial flows of silver into and out of the subcontinent,

commemorative: a coin issued often to honor an individual or an event—and which usually sells at a significant premium above the value of its contained metals.

bullion coin: a precious metals coin the price of which is based principally on the value of its metals content rather than its face value or legal-tender status—and which, unlike a commemorative, is bought and sold at only a small premium above the value of its gold, silver, or platinum content.

flows which in some years have had a profound effect on the world market for silver. In more recent years, domestic supplies have not been sufficient to satisfy local demand. As a result, a significant flow of silver has been smuggled into India—and this inflow reached a record 68 million ounces in 1992.

The group of countries consisting of former Soviet Union, Eastern Europe, and the remaining East Bloc nations (China and North Korea) is an important producer and consumer of silver. In line with the reported declines in the production of other metals and minerals—and in view of the general economic collapse—silver mine output in the former Soviet Union has fallen off sharply in the past few years.

Polish silver output—which is principally a byproduct of copper mining—has also fallen off in recent years. In contrast, China has enjoyed an improvement in its silver mine production from one year to the next over the past dozen years or so—and this pattern is expected to continue at least during the next 10 years.

Despite the contraction in mine production, reflecting the sharp cutback in domestic silver demand in the former Soviet Union and the improvement in secondary supplies from recycling, this group of countries could become an exporter of silver again to the world market, beginning in the middle 1990s.

THE MARKET BALANCE

Despite a significant improvement in silver's supply/demand balance since the middle 1980s, the metal's price has remained under pressure in recent years. Typically, commodity analysts interpret tightening supply and demand fundamentals and the establishment of a market deficit as a precursor of price appreciation.

For silver, today's deficit is a symptom of the metal's diminished role as a monetary medium and investment asset. In recent years, investors—frustrated and disenchanted with the metal's performance and prospects—have sought to reduce their total holdings of silver. In order to achieve this, the market has been pushed into deficit by persistent and aggressive investor sales. These sales have resulted in a lower market price for silver and have altered the entire supply/demand picture.

CHAPTER 11

Platinum and Palladium

*P*latinum group metals (PGMs) are a group of six distinct metals that are usually found in the same ore and that have generally similar chemical and physical properties. They are platinum, palladium, rhodium, iridium, ruthenium, and osmium. Of the six, only platinum (which is the most abundant of the six) and palladium (which is the next most abundant) are readily accessible to the average investor—through the purchase of physical metal, through futures contracts on the *New York Mercantile Exchange (NYMEX)*, and through the purchase of South African platinum mining equities.

Although platinum and palladium have largely industrial use, their status as precious metals and the similarity in their price performance with the price of gold, and their strong long-term market fundamentals have made these two metals increasingly popular among investors. Some investors have even begun buying platinum as a substitute for gold as hedge assets. Moreover, the ever-present threat to supplies due to the fact that South Africa and

platinum group metal (PGM): any of a number of related metals usually found in the same ore as coproducts or byproducts. In addition to platinum itself, the PGMs include palladium, rhodium, ruthenium, iridium, and osmium.

New York Mercantile Exchange (NYMEX): the world's leading future exchange trading platinum and palladium futures.

79

[handwritten margin notes: 1) Car converters 2) Jewelry → 80% in JAPAN]

Russia are the leading suppliers of PGMs may make these metals especially interesting at times.

PLATINUM AND PALLADIUM USES

Total industrial (noninvestment) demand for platinum amounted to some 3.5 million ounces in 1993. Platinum's single-largest consumer is the world auto industry which accounts for about 35 percent to 40 percent of total western world demand. Jewelry manufacturers are the second most important end-use sector, claiming about 30 percent to 35 percent of annual demand in recent years—and most of this, about 80 percent—is in Japan. In addition, the chemical, electronic, glass, and petroleum industries are also important users of platinum.

Worldwide palladium demand—excluding investment—has been running around 3.3 million to 3.5 million ounces per annum in recent years. By far, the electrical industry is the biggest end-use sector taking about one out of every two ounces of palladium each year. Dental use accounts for another 25 percent. Autocatalysts, jewelry, and a variety of less important applications take the rest.

Today, PGM-based *catalytic converters* are the only viable technology for limiting polluting automotive emissions. Among the countries that have legal limitations on polluting auto emissions are the United States, Canada, Mexico, Brazil, the 12 European Community nations, Austria, Switzerland, Norway, Sweden, Japan, Taiwan, and Australia.

Most auto companies now use three-way catalytic converters to control the three regulated polluting emissions: carbon monoxide, nitrogen oxides, and hydrocarbons. Typically, the three-way converters

catalytic converters: the air pollution control devices that are mandatory equipment on automobiles in the United States and in many other countries. Platinum and palladium serve as catalysts in the conversion of harmful and illegal air pollutants often found in auto exhaust into nonharmful emissions.

Table 11.1.   Platinum Supply and Demand Balance (thousands of ounces)

	1987	1988	1989	1990	1991	1992	1993[a]
Mine production							
South Africa	2,520	2,580	2,620	2,760	2,770	2,750	2,975
North America	140	210	195	185	220	200	195
Other market economies	40	50	60	65	70	120	125
Total	**2,700**	**2,840**	**2,875**	**3,010**	**3,060**	**3,070**	**3,295**
Secondary supply	225	250	265	285	240	270	290
East Bloc sales							
Russian exports	400	440	550	720	1,100	750	450
Other imports	30	40	40	0	−20	0	20
Total net sales	370	400	510	720	1,120	750	430
Total Supply	**3,295**	**3,490**	**3,650**	**4,015**	**4,420**	**4,090**	**4,015**
Industrial demand							
Japan	1,330	1,510	1,630	1,745	1,780	1,755	1,825
North America	915	915	995	960	940	830	950
Western Europe	495	490	565	665	750	825	935
Other	175	225	255	345	390	380	450
Total Industrial Demand	**2,915**	**3,140**	**3,445**	**3,715**	**3,860**	**3,790**	**4,160**
Net Surplus or Deficit (−)	**380**	**350**	**205**	**300**	**560**	**300**	**−145**
Retail investment	215	330	130	100	175	145	180
Large bar demand[b]	275	300	30	100	240	110	150
Total identified investment	490	630	160	200	415	255	330
Other stocks[c]	−110	−280	45	100	145	45	−475

[a] APMA projections for 1993.
[b] Excludes CIS, East Bloc, and South Asia.
[c] Totals may not add due to rounding.

Source: American Precious Metals Advisors. Copyright 1993—American Precious Metals Advisors, Inc.

Table 11.2.   Palladium Supply and Demand Balance (thousands of ounces)

	1988	1989	1990	1991	1992	1993[a]
Mine production						
South Africa	1,105	1,150	1,230	1,270	1,260	1,275
North America	370	375	370	420	400	400
Other market economies	70	60	70	70	70	70
Total	**1,545**	**1,585**	**1,670**	**1,760**	**1,730**	**1,745**
Secondary supply	65	70	85	85	100	110
Russian exports	1,170	1,650	1,870	2,150	2,100	1,950
Total Supply	**3,315**	**3,235**	**3,540**	**3,910**	**3,830**	**3,805**
Industrial demand[b]						
Japan	1,535	1,515	1,530	1,800	1,780	1,775
North America	1,020	1,070	1,080	1,095	1,160	1,215
Western Europe	605	585	590	620	675	710
Other	175	170	215	275	285	295
Total Industrial Demand[c]	**3,335**	**3,340**	**3,415**	**3,710**	**3,900**	**3,995**
Net Surplus or Deficit (−)	**−20**	**−105**	**125**	**200**	**−70**	**−190**

[a] APMA projections for 1993.
[b] Excludes CIS, East Bloc, and South Asia.
[c] Totals may not add due to rounding.

Source: Johnson Matthey and American Precious Metals Advisors. Copyright 1993—American Precious Metals Advisors, Inc.

[handwritten margin note: Ford Motor No Platinum But Palladium]

contain either platinum, palladium, and rhodium or just a mixture of platinum and rhodium.

Various auto companies (beginning with Ford in December 1988) have announced the development of catalytic converters meeting government mandated requirements without the use of platinum but instead relying on palladium. These periodic announcements have usually dented the price of platinum and boosted the price of palladium. So far, however, there does not appear to be any real threat to platinum usage since the palladium-only catalysts use about 3.5 times more metal than platinum-based systems and, therefore, there is no cost advantage in the palladium-only converter. Moreover, any major substitution of palladium for platinum would quickly alter the relative prices of the two metals, making the palladium-only system more expensive.

Growth in auto industry demand for these two metals is a big plus in the outlook for both of these metals. Not only should the number of vehicles manufactured from year to year continue to expand over the decade, but more countries will impose emission-control standards and many countries with environmental regulations already in place will further restrict emissions requiring the auto manufacturers to increase the PGM loadings in catalytic converters. Similarly, the likely expansion in the use of PGM catalysts to control emissions from stationary nonautomotive internal combustion engines is another potentially big growth sector for platinum and palladium.

Jewelry manufacturers are the next most important users of platinum and less important users of palladium. Japan alone, thanks to the uncommon popularity of platinum jewelry in this country, accounts for about 88 percent of all platinum jewelry manufactured and consumed. In recent years, Japanese consumers bought over one million ounces per year of platinum jewelry. As a result of this geographic concentration, platinum jewelry demand is especially sensitive to the economic situation and outlook in Japan as well as the yen-denominated price for the metal. Historically, lower prices in Japan—which may result from either an appreciation of the yen exchange rate or a decline in the dollar price of platinum—have prompted growth in jewelry demand.

PGMs are used by the electrical industry in contacts and conductors, in thin film circuits, and in thermocouples. Electronics is an especially important use of palladium, consuming about 1.7 million ounces or roughly 50 percent of the total demand. Palladium use in electronics has grown rapidly in the past dozen years prompted by substitution away from more costly gold and the recognition that palladium's physical characteristics are better suited in some electrical applications. In the chemical and petroleum industries, PGMs are used for their catalytic properties in the manufacture of a number of important chemicals (including nitric acid, a feedstock for many fertilizers, explosives, and plastics) and various petroleum refining processes. The trends toward growing use of heavy crudes and higher octane gasoline could increase demand for PGM catalysts. In the glass industry, platinum crucibles, bushings, and manufacturing equipment are indispensable because of the metal's high melting point and resistance to corrosion.

PLATINUM AND PALLADIUM SOURCES

Mine Production

Western world mine production of PGMs is concentrated in South Africa. This one country accounts for roughly 92 percent of platinum mine production (excluding the former and remaining East Bloc countries) and some 70 percent of total supplies—including market sales by these other

[handwritten margin notes: S. Africa 92% of Platinum Producers Excluding East Bloc countries CfS]

countries as well as scrap recovery. Similarly, about 73 percent of palladium mine output and about 34 percent of total world supply, including scrap and Russian sales, comes from South Africa. In all, South Africa's annual output of platinum and palladium are about 2.6 million ounces and 1.1 million ounces, respectively. Moreover, South African PGM output is concentrated with just two mining companies responsible for the bulk of production at a small number of underground mines. As a result, world platinum supplies are hostage not only to the political situation in that country but also the labor situation at any of the major mining facilities.

Next in importance as a supplier of PGM to the world market is Russia. Historically, the former Soviet Union's platinum sales amounted to between 200,000 and 400,000 ounces per year. But in the early 1990s, pressure to generate foreign exchange forced large-scale sales from industry/government stockpiles and annual platinum shipments reached as much as 1 million ounces in 1991. Russia is the single-largest supplier of palladium with shipments typically ranging from 1.2 million to 1.7 million ounces per year. But in 1989 through early 1992, the country's palladium sales were also inflated by stockpile sales. (As palladium sales returned to more normal rates in late 1992, world palladium prices rose from around $85 an ounce to over $115 before settling back toward the $100 per ounce level in mid-1993.)

Unlike the South African mines which produce primarily PGMs, Russian production is a byproduct of nickel-copper mining. Thus, demand and pricing of nickel and, to a lesser extent, copper are important determinants of Russian PGM mining. Russian

[handwritten margin notes: Kola Peninsula, Northern Urals, Near Finland, N/w. Siberia]

PGM mines are concentrated in the Noril'sk region of northwest Siberia and the Kola Peninsula near Finland with the former accounting for about 90 percent of the country's production. As with gold and other metals, mine output has fallen in recent years, reflecting labor problems, fuel shortages, and the overall deterioration throughout the economy. In particular, a lack of adequate capital investment and maintenance threatens further declines in PGM output in the mid-1990s.

[handwritten margin notes: Canada By Product]

Canada also produces PGMs—about 150,000 ounces of platinum and 200,000 ounces of palladium annually—as byproducts of nickel mining by Inco and Falconbridge. (Equity investors should note that the contribution of PGMs to these companies' revenues and profits is not large enough to make their stock prices sensitive to platinum and palladium prices.) In the United States, the Stillwater Mine in Montana is a primary producer of platinum and palladium with output of approximately 70,000 ounces of palladium and 30,000 ounces of platinum per year. Jointly owned by Johns-Manville and Chevron, the Stillwater Mine does not offer opportunities to the equity investor for exposure to these metals.

Secondary Supply

PGMs are now routinely recovered from scrapped automobile catalysts. By the early 1990s, nearly 200,000 ounces of platinum and 85,000 ounces of palladium emanated from recycling of junked automobiles. Additional amounts of these two metals are recovered from electronics, other industrial, and dental scrap as well as from old jewelry.

The supply of secondary platinum and palladium is in part a function of the price of these metals as well as the supply of scrapable material. Future growth in secondary supply will be related principally to the usage of these metals by the world auto industry—that is, the number of cars each year that are fitted with catalytic converters and the average loading of these metals per converter. Reflecting the buildup in European use of autocatalysts in the late 1980s and early 1990s, a significant rise in platinum and palladium scrap recovery should begin in the mid-1990s. Similarly, increased loadings of PGMs in the United States in the mid-1980s is already beginning to affect scrap supplies. In the United States, the average life of an auto prior to scrapage is seven years, but only about 70 percent of these are dismantled with the converters removed for PGM recovery. A higher price would undoubtedly boost the recovery rate.

Government Stockpiles

Another potential influence on the price of platinum and palladium are possible changes in the U.S. national defense stockpile. The U.S. government currently holds an inventory of 13,673 kilograms (439,600 ounces) of platinum and 39,265 kilograms (1.26 million ounces) of palladium. These existing stockpile levels are well below the recommended goals—40,745 kilograms of platinum and 66,873 kilograms of palladium. This suggests that in the future the U.S. government might make purchases of these metals to raise inventories toward stockpile goals. However, federal government budget cutting and an end of the cold war makes additional purchases extremely unlikely. Indeed, a re-evaluation and reduction in both goals and actual inventories could result in government sales in future years.

THE MARKET BALANCE

Reflecting the sizable increase in platinum and palladium sales by the former Soviet Union and the weakness in the world auto industry both platinum and palladium fundamentals deteriorated in the early 1990s with large surpluses in each market. Platinum was also especially affected by the softness in the Japanese platinum jewelry sector.

By late 1992, Russian shipments of these metals were beginning to fall back toward more normal rates. These supplies should diminish further in the mid-1990s reflecting the depletion in Russian inventories, reduced mine production, and an eventual pickup in domestic demand. And, by the mid-1990s, demand should be improving along with a recovery in the world and Japanese economies. These prospective trends suggest to many PGM analysts that the prices of these metals are likely to appreciate in the years ahead.

CHAPTER 12

Special Vehicles for Investing in Precious Metals

Precious metals investors have, by far, the widest choice of investment vehicles ranging from physical metal in a variety of forms to mining equities to options and futures. Ownership of physical metals is often the least risky but also the least leveraged. With equities, although you have additional leverage, you are also subject to a host of additional risks not related to the price of the underlying metal. These risks relate to the company, its management, its mines and their locations, and other factors that are discussed in the chapter on mining equities. *Futures contracts*, like physical metal, entail only price risk—but this is greatly magnified by their leveraged nature. *Options*—though often touted as limiting risk—entail all the risks of the underlying instrument and, as discussed in the chapter on options, it is very easy to lose your entire investment.

As with any investment, when buying and selling precious metals assets make sure that you are

futures contracts: *agreements between buyers and sellers of a commodity or financial asset setting the transaction price, quantity, and acceptable grade of material for delivery on some specified future date.*

options: contracts giving the buyer the right to take delivery (in the case of a call option) or make delivery (in the case of a put option) of a commodity or financial asset at a preset price on some specified future date. The seller of the option has the obligation to make delivery (in the case of a call option) or take delivery (in the case of a put option) if delivery is requested by the purchaser of the option.

bullion coins: coins that are valued only for their gold, silver, or platinum content rather than their face value and legal-tender status.

doing business with a reputable dealer or broker. Whether you are interested in coins, equities, futures, or options you should probably deal with a major national Wall Street firm, that is, unless you already have a trusting relationship elsewhere.

PHYSICAL OWNERSHIP— BULLION COINS

The safest way to invest in gold, silver, platinum, or palladium is to own the metal outright. As an investor, you are not likely to make a killing through physical ownership, but neither are you likely to lose your shirt. Except for palladium, one of the simplest and safest forms of ownership is *bullion coins.* A number of governments issue legal tender precious metals coinage. Typically, minted in one-ounce and fractional sizes, the prices of these coins are based on the underlying metal price plus a small premium. Australia has introduced larger sized bullion coins in two-ounce, ten-ounce, and kilogram weights. In contrast, *numismatic* or *commemorative coins* are purchased by collectors or investors betting on a rise in their scarcity value.

The popular bullion coins will trade at a small premium over their metal content. The wholesale prices of the top gold coin brands, for example, are all 3 percent over their gold value for the 1 ounce coins. The retail price to you, however, will generally run from 5 percent to 10 percent over the current market price of gold, depending on the dealer with whom you do business, the quantity of coins purchased, and other fees or commissions that may be charged to you. In addition, bullion coins—like other investments—trade at a bid-and-ask spread so that what you pay may be a fraction of a percent more than what you would receive for the coins at resale, assuming no change in the underlying gold price.

Bullion coins have a number of advantages over other forms of physical metal ownership. First, the major brands are very liquid—which means that they are extremely easy to buy and, more importantly, resell. Second, they are easy to store, easy to transport, and internationally tradable. Third, they are difficult to counterfeit—so it's virtually impossible for a professional to be fooled by a fake and there should be no need for a costly *assay* when you resell them. And, fourth, since they are fabricated in one-ounce, multiple-ounce, and fractional weights it is fairly easy to calculate the value of your investment at any time.

numismatic coins: coins that are valued by investors and collectors because of their rarity as well as their esthetic, cultural, or historical appeal rather than their metal content or face value.

assay: a chemical or physical analysis of ore, scrap, alloys, and other precious metals containing materials to determine its exact metal composition as well as its various mineral and chemical components.

BARS AND BULLION ALTERNATIVES

Bullion coins are good vehicles for many precious metals investors—particularly if the quantities don't number more than a few hundred ounces.

Table 12.1.   The Popular Bullion Coins

	Coin	Issuer
Gold	Eagle	United States
	Philharmonic	Austria
	Nugget	Australia
	Krugerrand	South Africa
	Maple Leaf	Canada
Silver	Eagle	United States
	Nugget	Australia
	Maple Leaf	Canada
Platinum	Koala	Australia
	Noble	Isle of Man
	Maple Leaf	Canada

There are, however, several alternatives that may be more convenient or efficient for investors buying large quantities.

Among the choices are bullion bars and wafers of various sizes and a variety of bullion proxies including storage accounts, accumulation programs, certificates, *warehouse receipts,* and bank-financed collateralized purchases that offer additional leverage. Generally larger bars and bullion proxies carry lower premiums than bullion coins and small bars and are, therefore, preferable to large-scale investors.

The most popular bar sizes are *kilobars* and 100-ounce bars for gold and platinum and 100-ounce and 1000-ounce bars for silver. Whatever size may be appropriate for your investment budget, make sure you buy a brand that qualifies as *good delivery* on COMEX (for gold and silver) and NYMEX (for platinum). Each bar will be stamped with the name of the fabricating refiner as well as a serial number and its exact weight. Buying a good delivery brand will assure that the bar can be easily resold.

warehouse and warehouse receipts: an exchange approved facility for holding metals or other commodities that are traded on a futures exchange. Warehouse receipts are issued representing ownership of the metal and satisfy an exchange's delivery requirements. See depository.

kilobar: a gold bar weighing exactly one kilogram or 32.1507 troy ounces.

good delivery: bars that meet the standards—purity, weight, shape, brand, etc.—of a given exchange or market association.

DELIVERY ISSUES

Many investors who purchase bullion or bullion coins wish to take actual delivery of their metal for storage in their own bank safe deposit facility or under the proverbial mattress. Remember, the contents of a safe deposit box are generally not insured by either the bank or federal government. Make sure that you arrange for insurance. Often this can be done simply by adding a rider to your homeowners or household insurance policy.

If you do take delivery of bullion or coins, it's usually best to arrange for storage with a recognized precious metals depository (such as Wilmington Trust in Delaware). Generally, if your metal is delivered directly to such a facility and never leaves its safekeeping custody, you will be able to resell your gold, silver, platinum, or palladium without incurring the cost of an assay. Most banks, brokerage houses, and leading precious metals dealers routinely deliver to recognized depositories.

Better yet for many investors are storage accounts and certificate programs. Many brokers and banks will offer one or both of these facilities. Often the only difference is the form of documentation you receive attesting to your ownership position. In a storage program, your metals ownership position may simply be indicated on your regular monthly or quarterly statement. With a certificate, you will generally receive a piece of paper that looks something like a stock certificate attesting to your ownership.

In either case, the metal that you purchase may be either specific bars or coins that belong to you or your holdings may be commingled with those of other investors. The advantage of the latter is that it allows investments in fractional units (often hundredths of an ounce) corresponding to a given dollar amount invested. For example, you could invest $5000 in palladium and receive a statement indicating that you own 47.62 ounces (which would be your share of a 50- or 100-ounce bar), a portion of which would be owned by other investors.

Accumulation accounts are another variant offered by banks and brokers that provide a facility for periodic—usually monthly—purchase of a fixed dollar amount of one metal or another, much like a payroll savings or investment plan allows employees to save or to buy company stock on a regular

accumulation plans: an investment plan offered by some brokerage firms allowing customers to invest a fixed dollar amount every month in metals, equities, or other investment products. While the dollar value of the investment remains the same, the quantity of metal or number of shares purchased on behalf of the investor varies depending on the current price of the asset. This method of investing is called dollar-cost averaging.

dollar-cost averaging: an investment technique requiring the purchase of a fixed dollar amount of a given asset—such as gold or mining shares—every week, month, or quarter.

depository: a bank or other institution that stores metal on behalf of investors. A number of depositories are selected by a futures exchange as approved storage locations for metal that may be delivered against futures contracts. Often the term is used to refer to precious metals storage facilities while non-precious metals and other commodities traded on futures exchanges are held in warehouses.

basis. In this case, you instruct your broker or banker to make a periodic debit from your checking or money market account and invest these funds at the current market price in the precious metal(s) of your choice.

Accumulation plans are a convenient way to *dollar-cost average* your purchases. By investing a fixed dollar amount on a regular basis, you will buy more ounces when the price is low and fewer ounces when prices are high. Metal purchased in an accumulation plan will be stored on a commingled basis with that of other investors.

Whether you are purchasing metal through a storage, certificate, or accumulation program, make sure that your purchase is actually held in a reputable *depository* and is not just a bookkeeping liability of the bank or broker without actual physical metal specifically allocated to your account.

PART 4

INVESTMENT CHOICES

CHAPTER 13

The Basics of Futures Markets

Futures markets offer metals investors and speculators great profit potential. Savvy traders and speculators have made fortunes participating in futures markets. But for the average investor, trading metals futures contracts can be risky business—and many will lose big money in this arena. The potential for both big gains and equally as big losses arises from the leveraged nature of futures contracts.

For most metals investors, equities, *options on futures* (discussed later), and—in the case of precious metals—physical ownership of the actual metals are much more sensible. But if you're willing to take risks and follow some common sense trading guidelines, futures markets can be exciting and rewarding.

The Commodity Exchange Inc. (COMEX) in New York and the New York Mercantile Exchange (NYMEX) are the two principal commodity futures exchanges in the United States where metals are traded. Gold, silver, copper, and aluminum trade on the COMEX while platinum and palladium trade

leverage: in futures and options markets, the ability to control an investment—the market value of which is a multiple of one's actual cash investment. Futures are leveraged because the investor pays only initial margin which is usually 5% or 10% of the contract's full value. Similarly, the premium paid on an option is only a fraction of the value of the underlying asset. Equities purchased on margin are leveraged for the same reason. However, in reference to equities—especially mining stocks—leverage may refer to the degree of price volatility of the stock price relative to the price of the metal or metals mined by the company.

on the NYMEX. This chapter is an introduction to trading metals on these *futures exchanges*. The investor new to commodities trading, however, is strongly advised to do more reading. Get the literature provided by the exchanges themselves and read a book or two that provides more information and advice on commodities trading. Then begin small—and make sure you have a good broker who can provide honest and sound advice as you learn the ropes.

NOT JUST FOR INVESTORS AND SPECULATORS

Thanks to the movies—and the unfortunate experiences of countless naive investors—futures exchanges have the reputation of a high-stakes gambling casino. But commodities futures have little in common with Las Vegas and Atlantic City. Futures trading was established to serve the commercial needs of many businesses that either produce, process, or consume metals and other commodities. Miners, refiners, dealers, and industrial users utilize futures markets for *hedging* their price risks. Futures contracts provide these businesses with a mechanism for locking in the price at which they will either buy or sell a given quantity of metal at some time in the future. For example, a manufacturer of copper electrical components may be required to quote selling prices for his products some 6 or 12 months before the parts are actually fabricated. He needs to know what his raw materials will cost in advance. By purchasing contracts for future delivery of copper on the COMEX, the

repurchase his position while the buyer will resell his position. For the speculator, the difference between the original purchase or sale price and the price of the offsetting trade to close out the position represents the realized profit or loss. For the hedger, the difference between these prices will offset the gain or loss that was incurred on the actual commodity. Less than 5 percent of all futures contracts traded on U.S. commodity exchanges ever result in delivery of the underlying commodity.

UNDERSTANDING FUTURES PRICES

Typical futures price tables, much as you'd expect to find in *The Wall Street Journal, Barron's*, and many other newspapers, contain the following information. At the top of each section is the metal and an abbreviation for the exchange on which it is traded—CMX for COMEX and NYM for New York Mercantile Exchange or NYMEX; the quantity of metal in ounces or pounds represented by one contract; and the price units—dollars per ounce, cents per ounce, or cents per pound.

Prices are reported for each contract month traded on the exchange and the contract months are listed in the left-hand column. Next to each month, the day's opening, high, low, and *settlement* (or closing) *prices* are reported along with the change from the prior day's settlement. In addition, the highest and lowest price recorded since trading for delivery in the given contract month first began are also reported.

The final column shows the *open interest* for each contract month. Open interest is the total number of

settlement price: often referred to as the closing price, this is the price set at the close of each trading day for every listed contract month on a futures exchange by the exchange's settlement committee. This price is the basis for determining margin calls by the clearinghouse.

open interest: the number of outstanding contracts on futures and options exchanges which remain "open"—that is which have not been closed out by opposite transactions or by delivery.

contango: on precious metals futures markets, the price relationship between nearby and more distant delivery months in which contract prices rise from month to month as the maturities to delivery increase.

arbitrage: the simultaneous buying and selling of the same asset in two different markets, exchanges, or locations in order to profit from small discrepancies in prices.

backwardation: the price relationship between nearby and more distant delivery months in which contract prices fall from month to month as the maturities to delivery increase.

contracts that have been entered into by buyers and sellers that have not yet been liquidated either by offsetting futures transactions or by actual delivery. Each open contract represents the long position of one trader (who has agreed to buy the commodity) and the short position of another trader (who has agreed to sell the commodity).

Along the bottom of each table is an estimate of the volume of contracts traded for the day, the actual number of contracts traded the previous day, and the total *open interest* for all contract months.

For the precious metals, notice that the settlement prices for each consecutive contract month are slightly higher than for the preceding month. This rising price trend is called the *contango*. For gold and silver, the contango or price difference between two contract months generally represents the cost of financing, storing, and insuring the metal for the time interval between the delivery dates of the two contract months. When actual futures prices diverge even slightly from these costs, arbitrage by bullion dealers and traders will always move the prices back to the appropriate relationship.

For copper and aluminum, the prices for future delivery generally represent the supply and demand for the metal in each delivery month. Sometimes prices for the nearby contract months may be higher than the prices for the more distant months (in contrast to the contango relationship which holds true for gold and silver). This occurs when there is a shortage of physical supplies currently available for immediate delivery or when market participants anticipate a big increase in supply relative to demand during the future months. When prices for the nearby contracts are higher than for the more distant contracts the market is said to be in *backwardation.*

THE CLEARINGHOUSE

In the course of trading on commodity exchanges such as COMEX and NYMEX, thousands of contracts are opened by prospective buyers and sellers of an assortment of metals. Keeping track of all of these contracts—processing all trades and assuring that sufficient margin is deposited by all participants to guarantee the integrity of the exchange and assure fulfillment of all contractual obligations by the exchange members and participants—is the job of the *clearinghouse*. The clearinghouse is responsible for keeping track of every trade on the exchange and matching up the brokerage firms representing the actual buyers and sellers in every transaction.

At the close of every trading day, the clearinghouse notifies its member firms of their net margin requirements based on all of the long and short positions of each firm's customers. In turn, each brokerage house keeps track of its own customers trades, net positions, and total margin due.

When contracts remain open until the delivery date, the clearinghouse also handles the notices of intentions to make delivery on behalf of the holders of short positions from each firm. These notices of intent to deliver are given to those member firms which, according to its records, have held their long positions for the greatest length of time. Each brokerage firm, in turn, assigns these *delivery notices* to its own customers with the oldest outstanding long contracts.

clearinghouse: an independent agency associated with futures and options exchanges charged with the responsibility of matching all buy and sell transactions and collecting margin on all open contracts. The clearinghouse—because it holds the good-faith margin deposits of all participants—guarantees the integrity of the exchange.

MARGIN ON FUTURES

Futures trading offers the potential for great profit and equally great loss because of the leveraged nature of the transaction. The investor or speculator entering into a contract to buy or sell is required to pay only a good faith deposit known as *margin*. The prospective buyer is not actually paying for the metal represented by the futures contract, nor is the seller receiving any advance payment. Indeed, the seller, just like the buyer, makes an initial margin payment. These margin payments are made to the respective brokerage firms which are acting on behalf of the buyer and seller. The brokerage houses, in turn, are required to deposit margin with the clearinghouse on the net outstanding positions of all of their customers.

Margin on futures transactions is a "good faith" deposit akin to a performance bond guaranteeing that the buyer or seller will fulfill the terms of the contract. In contrast, margin on equity transactions is a down payment on the actual purchase of an equity, with the broker extending credit to cover the balance due. In a margined equity transaction, the investor has purchased stock on credit and pays interest to the brokerage firm that has lent the necessary funds. But, since the futures market participant is not actually buying the underlying metal or commodity nor is he borrowing any funds from the broker, there is no credit being extended and no interest to be paid to the broker.

On U.S. futures exchanges—including COMEX and NYMEX—the margin requirements are set by the exchanges based on the recent price volatility of the particular metal. Margin payments are intended

margin: on commodity futures contracts, unlike margin on equities, is a good-faith deposit intended to assure that both parties to the contract— buyer and seller— perform as required by the contract. In contrast, margin on equities is a partial down payment with the balance of monies due on loan from the investor's stockbroker.

margin call: a request from a broker for additional funds in order to raise the cash position back to minimum levels after an adverse price move on futures or equity markets.

to cover any likely loss by an adverse daily price movement. Margin deposits are adjusted daily to reflect the most recent day's price change. For example, if the price moves against the investor's position, the broker will require payment of additional variation margin. Similarly, if the price changes in favor of the investor's position your margin account will be credited for the increased value of your contracts. These credits can be withdrawn as cash profits without selling out the position—or they can be used by an aggressive speculator to acquire additional futures positions in the hope of *pyramiding* past gains into spectacular profits.

pyramiding: the use of the appreciated value of futures contracts to finance the margin required for the acquisition of additional futures positions.

One of the important aspects of futures markets is that they provide a mechanism for speculators to profit equally from both rising and falling prices. A bullish investor or speculator can go long—betting that the price will rise—by entering into a contract to take future delivery of the underlying metal. Or he can go short—betting that prices will fall—by contracting to make delivery.

A Typical Transaction

Here are the steps in a hypothetical transaction in which the speculator believes that the price of platinum will rise over the next few months. First, the speculator calls his broker—usually one that specializes in futures markets, rather than his stockbroker—with instructions to enter into 10 contracts each representing 50 ounces of platinum for delivery in 6 months.

Assume at the time of the transaction, the price of platinum for delivery 6 months hence is $375 per ounce. These 10 contracts altogether total 500 ounces so their current value and cost to the speculator will be $187,500.

Although this is a big investment, the low margin requirements mean that the speculator will have to make an initial margin payment of perhaps only 5 or 10 percent of the total value. In this case, the broker requires a 10 percent margin payment of $18,750.

In this illustration, the speculator's intuition proves correct and the price of platinum moves higher day by day. After a few weeks, the metal's price has moved from $375 an ounce to $395—a gain of $20 an ounce. But the value of the 10 contracts has increased from $187,500 to $197,500—a gain of $10,000.

Now the investor has three choices: First, he can elect to take his profits, calling his broker with instructions to sell immediately at $395. A few days later a check arrives in the mail for $28,750 less commissions. In a matter of weeks, this wise or lucky speculator nearly doubled his money, thanks to the leveraging available through futures markets and the low initial margin that was required to "control" a fairly sizable investment.

If the investor believes that platinum is still likely to move higher, he can leave his position alone and let his profits accumulate if he is right and the metal continues to appreciate. If the market reverses, the gains can quickly evaporate. For the moment, however, the investor chooses to withdraw from his brokerage account the excess margin that has accumulated. At their current value, the 10 percent margin requirement means that the investor must have on deposit a good-faith payment of $19,750—but with the $10,000 gain his account is up to $28,750 and he can withdraw $19,000.

The aggressive speculator has a third choice—to use these additional funds to buy additional long futures positions. He instructs his broker to enter into 5 new contracts at $395 an ounce. Their total value is $98,750 requiring initial margin of $9,875, still leaving an excess balance in his margin account. Now the investor has 15 platinum futures contracts—and his profits on any price rise will be that much bigger. As long as the market continues to move higher, the aggressive investor can continue to pyramid his position by using existing gains to finance the margin on additional positions.

TRADING FUTURES

The day-to-day volatility of prices for many metals in combination with the leverage afforded by the low minimum margin requirements makes commodity futures a risky medium for many metals investors and speculators. Even with a correct forecast of price trends over the medium to longer term, an investor can quickly lose his initial margin—and more if he makes additional margin payments—by an adverse short-term price movement.

Most successful commodities traders rely on *technical analysis*—the study of past price movements and chart patterns—for a guide to short-term price prospects. Technical analysts often examine other market statistics, such as open interest and trading volume, along with actual price data. The investor planning to speculate in commodities markets should first read up on technical analysis

technical analysis: the examination of historical price movements for insight into future market action.

and become proficient at this art. But even those with a longer term perspective can benefit from a careful "reading of the charts" for clues to market timing and price turning points.

Markets are dynamic and quickly changing so the successful trader needs to be flexible and quickly adapt to the latest circumstances. In addition, since the nonprofessional participant in futures markets cannot pay constant attention to his investment, he needs to be familiar with the various methods of placing buy and sell orders with his broker in order to minimize the risks of adverse price fluctuations.

CHAPTER 14

The Basics of the London Metal Exchange

The London Metal Exchange (or LME), like U.S. futures markets, provides a forum in which investors and speculators can take positions in a variety of metals. The main differences—apart from its location—are the metals that are traded and the specific mechanics and vocabulary of the exchange.

In both cases, trading of futures contracts and options provide the investor and speculator significant leverage to changes in metals prices. You need to be aware that the opportunity to make big money is matched by the potential for loss.

While speculators may be important participants in LME trading, the exchange was founded in 1877 by merchants dealing in world metals markets to provide a mechanism for buying and selling metals that were shipped from foreign ports but had not yet arrived in London. And commercial participants— metals dealers, refiners, miners, and industrial users—today remain important traders on the LME, utilizing the market to lock in fixed purchase or sales prices in order to hedge against disadvantageous price movements.

Six major base metals are traded on the London Metal Exchange. These are aluminum, copper, lead, nickel, tin, and zinc—all metals that have been discussed earlier in this book. Investors wishing to play these metals on the LME are cautioned first to find a U.S. broker familiar with dealings on this exchange, get the LME's own literature that explains the exchange's particular workings and mechanics, and to do the necessary homework on the metal's fundamentals and price prospects.

PRINCIPALLY A FUTURES MARKET

The bulk of trading on the London Metal Exchange is in futures contracts by individuals and companies—both speculators and hedgers—who neither wish to make or take physical delivery. Instead, as with futures contracts in the United States, at some time prior to the contract's maturity, each party will close out its position by effecting an opposite trade, that is, the seller will repurchase his position while the buyer will resell his position.

For the speculator, the difference between the original purchase or sale price and the price of the offsetting trade to close out the position represents the realized profit or loss. For the hedger, the difference between these prices will offset the gain or loss that was incurred on the actual commodity.

For each of the metals traded on the London Metal Exchange, the contract specifications may seem at first a bit awkward to the American investor. In particular, the quantities, units of weight, pricing, and even deliverable form are more British than American.

TRADING SPECIFICS

For example, copper is traded in contracts representing 25 metric tons of electrolytic copper in the form of either Grade A cathodes or Grade A wire bars weighing from 110 kilograms to 125 kilograms. Pricing is in pounds sterling per metric ton. *Delivery dates* are daily for three months forward, then every Wednesday for the next three months forward and then every third Wednesday of the month for the next 21 months—so, in all, 27 months forward are traded.

delivery date: the specified date when a commodity traded on an exchange must be delivered to fulfill the terms of the futures contract.

Aluminum (or aluminium to the British) is also traded in contracts representing 25 metric tons of high-grade primary aluminum in the form of ingots, T bars, or sows. Ingot weights may range from 12 kilograms to 26 kilograms each, the maximum permitted weight of a T bar is 675 kilograms and the maximum permitted weight of a sow is 750 kilograms. (In 1992, the LME introduced another contract for secondary aluminum alloy meeting certain international die-casting standards. Secondary aluminum is traded in 20-ton contracts.)

Zinc is traded in 25-ton contracts of special high-grade zinc in the form of slabs, plates, or ingots weighing not more than 55 kilograms each. Primary aluminum and zinc both trade in U.S. dollars for 27 months forward with the same delivery dates as copper.

Refined tin conforming to certain industry standards is traded in 5-metric-ton contracts. Deliverable tin must be in ingots or slabs weighing at least 12 kilograms but not more than 50 kilograms each. Contracts are priced in U.S. dollars per ton with delivery daily for 3 months forward, then every Wednesday for the next 3 months, and then the third Wednesday of every month for the next 9 months. Tin trades for a total of 15 months forward.

Refined lead in pigs weighing not more than 55 kilograms each is traded in 25-metric-ton contracts. Lead contracts on the LME are denominated in pounds sterling per ton and are deliverable according to the same schedule as for tin.

Finally, primary nickel conforming to certain standards is traded in the form of cathodes, pellets, and briquettes. Contracts represent 6 tons and are denominated in U.S. dollars per ton. Delivery dates coincide with those of tin and lead.

As you may have noticed, dealings on the London Metal Exchange are carried out in pounds sterling for copper and lead while aluminum, nickel, tin, and zinc trading is conducted in U.S. dollars. However, U.S. dollars (as well as pounds, Deutsche marks, and yen) are recognized as good currencies for settlement purposes for all of the metals traded on the exchange. As a result, LME contracts can be issued by LME brokers in any of the four currencies for each of the six metals. American investors, therefore, can trade copper and lead in U.S. dollars even though trading on the floor of the exchange is conducted in pounds.

In contrast to the continuous trading on American exchanges, LME trading is broken down into two sessions with each metal trading sequentially for 5 minute intervals. Each metal is traded twice during each of the two sessions. Following each session, all the metals trade simultaneously for a short period in what is known as *kerb trading*.

THE CLEARING SYSTEM

As in the United States, keeping track of every trade, matching buyers with sellers, and assuring that sufficient margin is deposited by all participants to guarantee the integrity of the exchange and assure fulfillment of all contractual obligations by the exchange members and participants is the responsibility of the clearinghouse. In the case of the LME, the clearinghouse is the London Clearing House (LCH) division of the International Commodities Clearing House Limited (ICCH). The ICCH is owned by six major British banks.

In order to guarantee the integrity of the exchange and insure that all participants meet their contractual obligations the LCH requires a good-faith payment in the form of margin. Initial margin is generally 10 percent of the value of the metal under contract, although your broker may set his own margin requirements at a higher percentage. In addition to requiring initial margin on all LME positions, the London Clearing House requires daily variation margin payments on all open contracts if the market price moves unfavorably against them.

The concepts of margin and leverage as well as more detailed discussions of futures trading have been covered in the preceding chapter.

kerb trading: on the LME, a brief period at the end of each trading session when all of the listed metals are traded simultaneously. Originally, the term referred to off-exchange trading conducted literally on the curb of the street.

CHAPTER 15

The Basics of Investing in Mining and Metals Equities

Metals and mining equities are excellent vehicles for most investors—beginners and pros alike—to take advantage of expected trends in metals prices. Once you have analyzed a particular metal market and feel confident about the metal's price prospects, buying stock in a mining or metal processing company is one of the simplest means of betting on the expected price trend.

But, remember, that investing in metals and mining shares is not the same thing as owning the metal outright. Many factors other than the future price trend of the metal itself can affect the price of a mining company stock. These include, among other things, company fundamentals such as mining costs, labor relations, management, *ore reserves*, and sometimes the risks of operating in foreign countries. Moreover, mining companies often produce more than one metal—and the price prospects will often differ from one metal to another.

ore reserves: that portion of a mining resource which has been discovered and delineated by actual sampling and analysis—and which can be profitably mined at current market prices for the metal.

In addition, metals and mining equities are subject to overall stock market risk, just like shares in any other company. In October 1987, when Wall Street and stock markets around the world crashed, mining equities fell just as sharply—even though the prices for many metals were unaffected. Even in less dramatic circumstances, mining equity prices may be influenced by the overall bull or bear market trend in aggregate stock prices. Investors looking for portfolio diversification through exposure to gold or other precious metals need to remember that owning gold stocks is not the same thing as owning the real thing.

UNDERSTANDING LEVERAGE

Mining shares often offer leverage to changes in metals prices. A small change in the price of copper or platinum, for example, can result in a large change in the stock prices of companies mining or processing the metal. But this sensitivity to underlying changes in metals prices works in both directions. An adverse move in the price of a metal may result in a large decline in the stock price of a mining company.

Leverage results from the relationship of mining costs to the market price received for a mine's output. As an example, let's look at a hypothetical copper mining company—Copminco Inc. It costs Copminco $0.75 to mine, refine, and market each pound of copper it sells including all of its administrative, exploration, labor, fuel, and other expenses. If the market price of copper is $1.00 per pound, Copminco earns $0.25 per pound of copper it produces and sells. At this time, Copminco is selling on the stock exchange for $8.50 a share.

But, the world economy is strong, copper is in great demand, and its price is rising. After a few months, this metal's price rises to $1.25 per pound— but Copminco's costs are unchanged at $0.75. Its profits have now risen to $0.50 for each pound of copper sold. Over the past few months, copper prices rose by 25 percent from $1.00 to $1.25 per pound. But, during the same period, its profits have risen by 100 percent from $0.25 to $0.50 per pound. Reflecting the doubling in profits, Copminco's share price could easily have appreciated by even more, say from $8.50 to $20 or $25 a share.

Had the price of copper fallen—perhaps because a glut of metal was caused by the opening up of several new large mines around the world—Copminco's stock price could have fallen precipitously. In this illustration, copper drops to $0.70 a pound on the free market, a 30 percent decline. Copminco's operating costs are still $0.75 for each pound of copper produced—so the company has gone from healthy profitability to a money-losing situation. In these circumstances, it would not be surprising to see its share price on the stock exchange fall from $8.50 to perhaps $2.00 or $3.00 a share.

COMPANY FUNDAMENTALS

Once you have analyzed the markets and have identified one or more metals that you think will be moving higher, you still need to pick the right companies in which to invest. Most investors, except the seasoned professional money manager who specializes in the mining sector, will need to rely on brokerage house security analysts, newsletter writers, and the investor relations departments of each mining company for the information necessary to make educated investment decisions.

For each mining company under consideration as a prospective investment, you will want to know about its management, its operating costs, its labor relations, and its *reserve life*. You will also need to know about any environmental and other regulatory issues that may affect the company's profitability. And, if it has operations abroad, country risk and foreign exchange prospects may also be relevant. As an investor, you will want to avoid companies that have a history of difficult labor relations, where environmental and regulatory costs are a problem, and where overseas operations are at risk because of unfriendly government relations.

reserve life: the number of years that a mine can continue producing at its optimal operating rate until its currently defined reserves are fully depleted.

Some investors don't pay enough attention to the quality of a mining company's management team. If you are a short-term investor looking for a quick gain or an expected run up in the underlying metal price, management may not matter too much. But if you have a medium-term to long-term perspective, the quality of management is crucial. Look for a well-rounded team, not just a company run by a couple of geologists. At the same time, make sure the management is not top heavy and overweight. One quick check is to compare head office administration costs (which you will find in each company's annual report statements) as a percentage of revenues from one company to the next within a particular metal mining sector. Apart from this, and the occasional magazine or newspaper article, it's hard for the amateur investor to assess management other

Break even cash production costs

than to rely on the opinions of securities analysts and newsletter writers.

Make sure you know the break-even *cash production cost*. Conservative investors generally favor companies with operating costs well below the current price received in the market for the mine's output. This way, an adverse price move in metal prices won't turn a profitable company into a losing one. But, a high-cost producer—a company where operating costs per unit of production are close to the current market price of the metal—provides more leverage to an expected move in metal prices.

Leverage

I. Production costs are generally related to such factors as the *ore grade* and metallurgy of the ore, the depth of mining, the hardness of the rock, the amount of waste material that must be removed along with the ore, possibly the location of the mine, labor costs, environmental regulations, and the degree of difficulty in mining.

II. Equally important are the company's ore reserves. How many years can mining continue at the current rate—and, importantly, is the company replacing depleted ore reserves through exploration and development activities? *Replacement of ore Reserves*

Ore is rock, gravel, clay, sand, and so on, from which a mining company can profitably extract a given metal. Reserves are designated as proven, probable, or possible, depending on the amount of exploration activity—drilling and sampling—that has been done by the mine's geologists. Securities regulators and accounting professionals have strict rules governing the designation of reserves.

To be proven, reserves must be defined by closely spaced drilling and sampling of the ore body. Since this can be expensive, mining companies usually

cash production cost: the cost of mining a given metal generally including milling, refining, and other direct production costs but usually excluding taxes, depreciation, financing, marketing and other indirect expenses. ✳

ore grade: usually reported in grams or kilograms per metric ton, is a measure of the metal content of a mine's ore body.

ore: any naturally occurring mineral containing one or more metals or other elements in such quantities and chemical combinations that their commercial extraction is profitable.

prove up just a few years of future production and add to proven reserves from year to year as existing reserves are mined out. However, securities analysts and company management will usually offer opinions about reserves and mine life.

SECURITIES ANALYSIS

It is often difficult to compare one mining company to another. Generally, the professional is seeking the company in a given mining sector that offers the best value—and, given the price outlook for the underlying metal and one's own investment objectives, is more leveraged, more conservative, and the safest company in the group, or somewhere in between. Apart from relative costs of production, a number of other indicators may be helpful.

price-earnings (P/E) ratio or multiple: a ratio in which a stock's current market price is divided by its past or prospective annual earnings. It is also a measure of the number of years it would take the company to earn its stock price.

Look to brokerage house analysts and the investment newsletters for earnings forecasts for the next few years. Check to make sure that the assumptions about the price prospects for the underlying metal are consistent with your own views. Then see which companies have the biggest increases in projected earnings in the next year or two.

Next, for the group of companies under consideration, compare the *price-to-earnings ratios* or *P/Es*. This ratio provides a means of measuring relative value. It tells you how much you are paying, in terms of current stock price, for a year of earnings. A high price-to-earnings ratio may indicate that a company is overvalued—or, simply, that it is a high-quality company that is worth more. In order to assess the meaning of a given company's P/E relative to other similar companies, you must know more about the company's fundamentals.

[Handwritten at top: market capitalization per unit of reserves / production]

Two additional ratios of relative value are market capitalization per unit of reserves and market capitalization per unit of production. Market capitalization is the total current value of the company's outstanding stock that can be calculated by multiplying the share price times the number of shares outstanding. The first ratio is a measure of how much you are paying when you buy the company's shares for its proven and/or probable reserves. The second ratio is an indicator of how much you are paying for each ounce or pound of annual production.

Finally, one of the handiest ratios is the payback period. This is the number of years it will take the mining company to earn its current share price at its current rate of production and at the current market price of the metal mined. The payback period can be calculated by dividing the market capitalization per ounce of production by the difference between the current metal price and the mine's operating cost per unit of production. Companies with shorter payback periods are often relatively better values.

*[Handwritten margin notes:
① Price per proven or probable Reserves.
② Price per oz of production.
* Payback period. (Number of years it will take the Co to earn its current share price at its current rate of production and at the current market price of the metal mined.)]*

SUMMING UP

Remember, investing in mining shares is not without risk. Not only are you accepting the risk of an adverse movement in the underlying metal—but you are subject to a variety of other company and stock market risks. One way to minimize company risk is to thoroughly understand and analyze each and every company that is under consideration. (Tables 15.1 and 15.2 list selected *nonferrous metals* and mining companies and selected precious metals companies, respectively.)

nonferrous metals: metals and alloys that do not contain iron or in which iron is only a minor constituent. Examples of nonferrous metals include copper, brass, bronze, tin, lead, aluminum, and zinc.

Table 15.1.   Selected Nonferrous Metals and Mining Companies

Company	Metals	Country	Exchange
Alcan Aluminum Ltd.	Aluminum	Canada	NYSE, TSE
Alcoa	Aluminum	US	NYSE
Asarco Inc.	Copper, Lead, Zinc, Silver	US	NYSE
Brunswick Mining & Smelting Corp.	Zinc, Lead, Copper, Silver	Canada	TSE
Cominco Ltd.	Zinc, Copper, Lead, Nickel	Canada	TSE
Cominco Resources Intl.	Copper, Nickel	Canada	TSE
Cyprus-Amax Minerals	Copper, Coal	US	NYSE
Freeport Copper and Gold	Copper, Gold, Silver	US	NYSE
Gibraltar Mines Ltd.	Copper, Molybdenum, Nickel	Canada	NYSE, TSE
INCO Ltd	Nickel, Copper, Gold	Canada	NYSE, TSE
Kaiser	Aluminum	US	NYSE
Magma Copper Co.	Copper	US	NYSE
Metall Mining Corp.	Copper, Zinc, Gold	Canada	TSE
Noranda Inc.	Copper, Zinc, Aluminum, Forest products, Oil & Gas	Canada	TSE
Phelps Dodge Corp.	Copper	US	NYSE
Princeton Mining Corp.	Copper, Gold, Silver	US	NYSE
Reynolds Metals	Aluminum	US	NYSE
Rio Algom Ltd	Copper, Oil & Gas, Coal, Gold, Uranium	Canada	TSE
Aberfoyle	Zinc, Lead	Australia	Sydney
Alcoa of Australia	Aluminum	Australia	Sydney
BHP	Multi-metallic, Oil & Gas, Steel	Australia	Sydney
Comalco	Aluminum	Australia	Sydney
MIM	Multi-metallic, Gold	Australia	Sydney
Pazminco	Zinc	Australia	Sydney
Western Mining	Aluminum, Nickel, Gold, Oil & Gas	Australia	Sydney
RTZ	Multi-metallic	United Kingdom	NYSE, London

Table 15.2. Selected Precious Metals Companies

Company	Metals	Country	Exchange
Agnico-Eagle	Gold, Silver	Canada	ASE, TSE
Amax Gold	Gold	US	NYSE
Barrick Gold	Gold	Canada	NYSE, TSE
Battle Mountain Gold	Gold	US	NYSE
Cambior	Gold, Other	Canada	ASE, TSE
Coeur d'Alene	Silver	US	NYSE
Echo Bay	Gold, Silver	Canada	ASE, TSE
Euro-Nevada	Gold finance	Canada	TSE
Franco-Nevada	Gold finance	Canada	TSE
FMC Gold	Gold	US	NYSE
Goldcorp	Gold, Other	Canada	ASE, TSE
Gold Reserve Corp.	Gold	Canada	TSE
Hecla Mining	Silver	US	NYSE
Hemlo Gold	Gold	Canada	TSE, ASE
Homestake	Gold	US	NYSE
Newmont Gold	Gold	US	NYSE
Newmont Mining	Gold	US	NYSE
Pegasus Gold	Gold	US	ASE, TSE
Penoles	Silver	Mexico	Mexico
Placer Dome	Gold, Silver, Other	Canada	NYSE, TSE
Rayrock Yellowknive	Gold	Canada	ASE, TSE
Royal Oak Mines	Gold	Canada	ASE, TSE
Teck	Gold, Copper, Coal, Zinc	Canada	NYSE, TSE
Venezuelan GoldFields	Gold	Canada	TSE
Viceroy Resource	Gold	US	ASE
Wharf Resources	Gold	US	ASE, TSE
ACM Gold	Gold	Australia	Sydney
Delta Gold	Gold	Australia	Sydney
Dominion Mining	Gold	Australia	Sydney
Emperor Mines	Gold	Fiji	Sydney
Gold Mines of Kalgoorlie	Gold	Australia	Sydney
Highlands Gold	Gold	Australia	Sydney
Homestake Gold	Gold	Australia	Sydney
Kidston	Gold	Australia	Sydney
Niugini Mining	Gold	Papua-New Guinea	Sydney
Newcrest Mining	Gold	Australia	Sydney
Normandy Poseidon	Gold	Australia	Sydney
Placer Pacific	Gold	Australia	Sydney
Renison Goldfields	Gold	Australia	Sydney

(continued)

Table 15.2. *Continued*

Company	Metals	Country	Exchange
Sons of Gwalia	Gold	Australia	Sydney
Western Mining	Gold	Australia	Sydney
Beatrix	Gold	South Africa	USOTC, Jo'burg, London
Buffelsfontein	Gold	South Africa	USOTC, Jo'burg, London
Deelkraal	Gold	South Africa	USOTC, Jo'burg, London
Dornfontein	Gold	South Africa	USOTC, Jo'burg, London
Driefontein	Gold	South Africa	USOTC, Jo'burg, London
Elandsrand	Gold	South Africa	USOTC, Jo'burg, London
Ergo	Gold	South Africa	USOTC, Jo'burg, London
Freegold	Gold	South Africa	USOTC, Jo'burg, London
Harmony	Gold	South Africa	USOTC, Jo'burg, London
Hartesbeestfontein	Gold	South Africa	USOTC, Jo'burg, London
Kinross	Gold	South Africa	USOTC, Jo'burg, London
Kloof	Gold	South Africa	USOTC, Jo'burg, London
Randfontein	Gold	South Africa	USOTC, Jo'burg, London
St. Helena	Gold	South Africa	USOTC, Jo'burg, London
Southvaal	Gold	South Africa	USOTC, Jo'burg, London
Unisel	Gold	South Africa	USOTC, Jo'burg, London
Vaal Reefs	Gold	South Africa	USOTC, Jo'burg, London
Western Areas	Gold	South Africa	USOTC, Jo'burg, London
Western Deep	Gold	South Africa	USOTC, Jo'burg, London

Table 15.2. *Continued*

Company	Metals	Country	Exchange
Winkelhaak	Gold	South Africa	USOTC, Jo'burg, London
Zandpan	Gold	South Africa	USOTC, Jo'burg, London
Anglo American	Gold finance	South Africa	USOTC, Jo'burg, London
Amgold	Gold finance	South Africa	USOTC, Jo'burg, London
Anglovaal	Gold finance	South Africa	USOTC, Jo'burg, London
ASA	Gold fund	US/South African	NYSE
Gencor	Gold finance	South Africa	USOTC, Jo'burg, London
Gold Fields of South Africa	Gold finance	South Africa	USOTC, Jo'burg, London
Johannesburg Consol. Invest.	Gold finance	South Africa	USOTC, Jo'burg, London
Rand Mines	Gold finance	South Africa	USOTC, Jo'burg, London
Impala	Platinum	South Africa	USOTC, Jo'burg, London
Northum	Platinum	South Africa	USOTC, Jo'burg, London
Rustenburg	Platinum	South Africa	USOTC, Jo'burg, London
Johnson Matthey	Platinum refiner & fabricator	United Kingdom	London

CHAPTER 16

An Introduction to Options on Equities and Futures

*O*ptions, whether on equities or futures, offer investors a good vehicle for speculating on prospective metals price movements. Options combine the opportunity for big profits with less risk than futures trading but more risk than either outright ownership of the metal or investing in mining equities. But you can easily lose your initial investment—so options are generally not for the conservative investor.

The best way to understand options is to review their history. Options had their birth in the real estate industry where in return for a cash payment a developer could purchase the right to buy a piece of property from the landowner at a preset price anytime during a contracted time period, perhaps a few months or years. If the developer chose not to acquire the property during the contracted time period, he lost only the initial cash cost of the option. From another perspective, the option gave the property owner a mechanism for generating some additional income on an otherwise idle piece of land.

Like the real estate option, options on metals and mining shares give potential buyers the opportunity to lock in a price on a prospective investment purchase for a period of time. At the same time, they offer the owners of these assets a vehicle for enhancing overall return.

An options contract is an agreement giving the buyer of the option the right but not the obligation to buy (or sell) an underlying asset within some prespecified timeframe at a predetermined price to the seller—also known as the *grantor* or *writer*—of the options contract. If the options buyer elects to exercise the option by demanding to buy (or sell) the underlying asset, the options seller is obligated to turn over (or accept delivery of) the asset at the predetermined price. An option which is not exercised during the specified timeframe simply expires without any remaining value.

In addition to exchange-traded equity options on a large number of mining stocks, options on gold and silver futures contracts are traded on COMEX. And, on the London Metal Exchange, options trade on copper, aluminum, lead, tin, zinc, and nickel.

TERMINOLOGY

An option granting the holder the right to buy the underlying asset is known as a *call* option. An option granting the holder the right to sell the underlying asset is known as a *put* option.

Options are identified by the name of their underlying asset, the option's expiration month, and its *strike price*. So, an option to sell 100 shares of

grantor: *the seller or writer of an option.*

call: *gives the investor the right—if he so chooses—to purchase the underlying asset at a preset price during the life of the options contract.*

put: *gives the investor the right to sell the underlying asset at a preset price during the life of the options contract.*

Homestake Mining at $12 a share between now and next April is known as a Homestake April 12 put. Similarly, an option to buy a COMEX futures contract representing 100 ounces of gold for delivery in July at $350 an ounce is called a COMEX July 350 call.

The predetermined price at which an option to buy or sell the underlying asset may be exercised prior to its expiration date is called the *strike price*. In the previous example, the strike price at which the owner of the option can buy 100 shares of Homestake Mining is $12. This price is set contractually when the investor first acquires the option and will not vary over the life of the option regardless of any variation in the price of Homestake Mining shares.

The cost of purchasing an option—the amount paid by the buyer to the seller or writer—is known as the *premium*. For exchange-traded options, this premium is determined by the actions of buyers and sellers on the floor of a stock or commodity exchange. The premium is the price the options buyer is willing to pay for the right to acquire the underlying asset at the predetermined strike price during the life of the options contract.

In theory, the options premium consists of two components—its *time value* and its *intrinsic value*. The intrinsic value—equal to the option's value at exercise—is the amount by which a call option's strike price is *below* the price of the underlying asset or the amount by which a put option's strike price is above the underlying asset price. Any option which has intrinsic value is *"in the money."*

An option is *"out of the money"* and without any intrinsic value when the strike price, in the case of a call, is above the market price of the underlying asset or, in the case of a put, when the strike price is

strike price: the predetermined contractual price at which an option may be exercised and the underlying asset bought (in the case of a call) or sold (in the case of a put). Also known as the exercise price.

premium: for a bullion coin or bar, the difference between the price paid for the item and the current market value of its metal content. In the options market, the price paid by the buyer to the seller of the option.

intrinsic value: the amount by which an option is in the money. An option which is not in the money has no intrinsic value.

time value: the amount by which an option's premium exceeds its intrinsic value. Time value reflects the amount of time remaining before the option matures as well as the price volatility of the underlying asset.

below the market price of the underlying asset. And, when the current market price of the underlying asset is equal to the option's strike price, the option is *"at the money."* In this case, the option also has no intrinsic value.

Sometimes an option's premium will exceed its intrinsic value. This excess, known as the time value, is the excess amount the buyer is willing to pay in the expectation that the intrinsic value will increase (i.e., the underlying asset price will appreciate) prior to expiration. This time value is related to:

in the money: when a call option's strike price is lower than the current market price of the underlying asset. A put option is "in the money" when its strike price is above the current market price of the underlying asset.

1. The time left until expiration—the more time, the greater the likelihood the underlying asset might appreciate. As the expiration date approaches, the time value will drop off quickly.
2. The price volatility of the underlying asset—the greater the volatility, the greater the chance that the underlying asset might appreciate, so high price volatility generally makes an option more expensive.
3. In the case of equity options, the expectation of any dividend that might be paid prior to expiration—since this is the amount that would be sacrificed by the investor owning an option rather than the underlying shares.
4. The interest rate and trading expenses related to owning the underlying asset—since this is the cost to arbitrageurs of profiting from differences between the theoretical premium and the actual cost of the option. Professional options traders rely on complex computer models to calculate the theoretical price of an option.

CALL OPTIONS—BETTING ON AN UPTREND

Call options are an excellent vehicle for speculating on an expected trend in the price of a given metal because they carry the potential for big gains. But don't kid yourself with the myth that there is limited risk in purchasing call options. If you're wrong in your expectations, your call will expire worthless and your loss will be 100 percent of your investment.

Let's say that you believe that the price of copper is set to rise. One way to profit from this expected trend would be to buy COMEX copper futures contracts, another would be to invest in the stocks of copper mining companies such as Phelps Dodge, Asarco, Magma Copper, or Cyprus Minerals—or you could buy call options on any of these stocks. Remember, just as in direct equity investment, options require a view not just of the underlying metal price but also of the particular company represented by the equity option.

A Typical Transaction

You've done your homework and you decide to speculate on expectations of a rise in the price of copper by purchasing call options on Cyprus Minerals. Cyprus Minerals July 40 calls are actively traded on the Chicago Board of Trade. A call giving you an option to buy 100 shares is trading at $^{12}/_{16}$ths (or 75 cents per share)—$75 per option. Cyprus Minerals stock is now at $34 so the options are out of the money. To profit from this transaction, Cyprus Minerals stock must rise above the strike price, the point at which the options go into the

out of the money: in options markets, refers to put options where the strike price is lower than the current market price of the underlying asset or call options where the strike price is higher than the current market price of the underlying asset.

at the money: an option market term describing the price point when the strike price and the current market price of the underlying asset are the same.

money, by an amount equal to the cost of the option plus any brokerage commissions on the trade.

Once the stock moves above the $41 level ($40 strike price plus 75 cents plus commissions), you will begin to profit dollar for dollar with any gains in the stock price. If you were correct in your underlying analysis about copper prices and Cyprus Minerals moved up to $45 a share, you would earn approximately $400 upon exercising your option on 100 shares ($45 share price minus $40 strike price minus 75 cents premium minus commissions times 100 shares).

So for a $75 investment, the cost of the option, your net gain would be about $400—not bad for a day's work. As you can see, buying out-of-the-money call options with low premiums offers the potential for significant profits if the market makes a big move in your favor. On the other hand, suppose your analysis or timing was wrong, copper prices barely rose or worse yet fell, and Cyprus Minerals stock price never reached the option's strike price of $40 by the July option's expiration date. In this case, the option would expire worthless and your initial investment of $75 would be forfeited.

BEAR MARKET PROFITS

Options also allow the investor/speculator the opportunity for handsome gains even in a bear market. Suppose your analysis suggested that copper prices were likely to fall. You could buy put options which rise in value as the price of the underlying asset depreciates. Again, as with calls, you could choose put options on COMEX copper futures or on a number of mining equities.

In this example, you choose to purchase put options on COMEX copper futures. Each COMEX copper futures contract represents 25,000 pounds of the metal. With copper prices at the time of writing near $1.00 per pound, each copper futures contract provides for eventual delivery, if exercised, of about $25,000 worth of copper. Typically, the speculator can purchase or sell one futures contract by depositing margin of only 10 percent to 15 percent of the contract value—in this case about $2500 to $3750. But if the price moves against his position, the investor/speculator is subject to virtually unlimited margin calls.

Instead of speculating directly in futures, you can limit your downside risk by utilizing options. In this example, you buy a put option which would require the seller or grantor of the option to purchase a futures contract at a predetermined price of copper should you choose to exercise your right to sell. A May 92 put has a strike price of 0.60 cents— so a put on one COMEX copper contract would cost $1500 (25,000 pounds times 0.60 cents per pound). In order to profit from this position, copper must fall at least 0.60 cents below the strike price by the May expiration date.

If the price fell to 89 cents per pound and you chose to exercise your option, your profit would be $600 (92 cents minus 0.60 cents minus 89 cents times 25,000 pounds) for each put option you purchased. If copper fell more sharply, say to 80 cents per pound, your profit would be $2,850 (92 cents minus 0.60 cents minus 80 cents times 25,000 pounds) for each option you purchased. If copper prices failed to fall below the strike price of 92 cents per pound your put would expire without any value and you would lose your initial investment of $1500.

OTHER OPTIONS STRATEGIES

Apart from offering the potential for big speculative gains, options can be useful to metals investors in other ways. For example, if you are bullish on the price prospects for a particular metal and have invested in the metal itself or a related equity or futures contract, you can hedge against a possible near-term price decline, if you expect a temporary setback, by purchasing a related put option. If the asset depreciates, the option appreciates offsetting all or part of the loss. The strategy is appropriate only when your analysis suggests that the metal price may be at risk in the short run, but you remain bullish and committed to your basis position in the long run.

Another strategy popular with many investors is the use of options to generate some additional income or return on the underlying asset. Here the investor, rather than buying puts or calls, sells or writes call options against an underlying asset which he already owns. If you own silver bullion or coins, for example, which offer no current yield in the form of interest or dividends, you might elect to write *covered calls*. Writers of covered calls receive income in the form of the premium paid by the buyer. In return, the writer is giving up the potential appreciation in his silver bullion position above the option's strike price.

Suppose you own 5000 ounces of silver. The current price is $3.75 an ounce. You sell (write) call options with strike prices of $4.25 on all 5000 ounces. The calls expire next September. You receive a premium from the buyer of the option of 25 cents per ounce or $1250. If between now and September the price of silver rises above the strike price of $4.25, the holder of the option will demand that you sell him the silver at $4.25 an ounce—so your gain was limited to 50 cents plus the 25 cent premium on each of the 5000 ounces. On the other hand, if silver does not rise above the strike price, you'll still own the silver—but you will have earned an extra 25 cents per ounce on your position.

In the jargon of the options world, a call is "covered" when you own the underlying asset and "naked" when you don't. Writing naked calls is an especially risky business because you could be required to purchase the underlying asset in order to make delivery. When you write calls, your broker will ask that the underlying asset be deposited with his firm to guarantee that you will make delivery if demanded by the options owner. Alternatively, if you write a naked call a margin payment will be required.

covered call option: if the writer or seller of a call option on metals, futures contracts, or equities owns the underlying asset and therefore can make delivery if required the option is covered. In contrast, a naked option is an option where the writer does not own the underlying asset.

SUMMING UP

Options on equities and futures contracts offer investors/speculators a fairly leveraged mechanism of profiting from expected movements in metals prices. Options are often touted because losses are limited to your initial investment—but, remember, losing 100 percent of your investment is a big price to pay if you are wrong in your assumptions about prospective metals prices.

APPENDIX
The Top 19 Metals

Metal	Symbol	Atomic Weight	Specific Gravity	Melting Point (Celsius)	Color
Aluminum	Al	26.97	2.7	658	Tin white
Chromium	Cr	52.01	7.19	1860	Greyish white
Copper	Cu	63.54	8.96	1083	Reddish orange
Gold	Au	197.2	19.32	1063	Yellow
Iron	Fe	55.85	7.9	1535	Greyish white
Lead	Pb	207.21	11.34	327	Blue grey
Magnesium	Mg	24.32	1.74	650	Silver white
Manganese	Mn	54.93	7.44	1244	White grey
Mercury	Hg	200.61	13.55	−38.87	White
Molybdenum	Mo	95.95	10.3	2620	Dull silver
Nickel	Ni	58.69	8.88	1455	White
Palladium	Pd	106.4	12.02	1552	White
Platinum	Pt	195.09	21.45	1769	White
Rhodium	Rh	102.91	12.4	1960	Bluish white
Silver	Ag	107.88	10.5	960	White
Tin	Sn	118.7	7.29	231.84	Bright white
Titanium	Ti	47.9	4.5	1680	Dark grey
Tungstun	W	184	19.3	3370	Steel grey
Zinc	Zn	65.38	7.2	419.5	Bluish white

Glossary

accumulation plans   an investment plan offered by some brokerage firms allowing customers to invest a fixed dollar amount every month in metals, equities, or other investment products. While the dollar value of the investment remains the same, the quantity of metal or number of shares purchased on behalf of the investor varies depending on the current price of the asset. This method of investing is called dollar-cost averaging.

actuals   refers to the actual metal as opposed to futures and forward contracts.

allocated metal   metal that is stored in a bank or metal depository in a segregated account belonging to a specific owner.

alloy   a mixture or combination of two or more metals, often to impart certain desired characteristics such as strength, conductivity, color, etc.

alumina   an oxide of aluminum often produced from bauxite ore as the first step in manufacturing aluminum.

aluminum bronze   an alloy of copper and aluminum containing roughly 90 to 95 percent copper and 5 to 10 percent aluminum, often used for seamless tubing and wire.

American Depository Receipt (ADR)   a certificate issued by American banks representing ownership of foreign securities to simplify U.S.

investment in overseas stocks. The issuing bank holds the actual securities in trust and the certificates trade on U.S. equity or over-the-counter markets.

apothecaries' weight   literally, the system of weights used by pharmacists. Precious metals are traditionally weighed in troy ounces which are units of the apothecary system. One troy ounce equals 31.1035 grams while a standard ounce equals 28.349 grams.

approved refiner   a commercial refiner whose branded bars (or product in other forms) are accepted as good delivery by one or another metals or futures exchange.

arbitrage   the simultaneous buying and selling of the same asset in two different markets, exchanges, or locations in order to profit from small discrepancies in prices.

assay   a chemical or physical analysis of ore, scrap, alloys, jewelry, bars, and other metal-containing materials in order to determine the exact metal content and the presence of other minerals and impurities.

at the money   an option market term describing the price point when the strike price and the current market price of the underlying asset are the same.

backwardation   a price situation on futures markets where the spot price for immediate delivery is above the price for delivery in the future. Backwardation usually occurs when there is a shortage of physical metal in deliverable form readily available in the market.

base metal   any of a number of non-precious metals that lose their metallic luster and readily tarnish at normal temperatures. Examples include iron, copper, lead, zinc, and nickel.

bauxite   hydrated aluminum oxide ($Al_2O_3 \cdot 2H_2O$), the principal ore from which aluminum is extracted.

blister copper   crude copper of roughly 99 percent purity. Blister copper is not of sufficient purity for most industrial applications.

brass   an alloy containing principally copper and zinc with other metals, especially tin, used in lesser proportions.

brazing brass   an alloy of 50 percent zinc and 50 percent copper with a low melting point.

bronze   a copper-rich alloy containing tin and sometimes small amounts of other minerals such as zinc or phosphorus.

bullion   refined bars or ingots of gold or silver, typically of high purity, which are traded, held by central banks and investors, and used as the raw material by jewelry manufacturers and other industrial users.

bullion coin   a precious metals coin the value of which is based on the current market price of its metals content rather than its face value and legal-tender status. Bullion coins are minted as investment media rather than as circulating currency and trade at a small stable premium over their metal content value. In contrast, "numismatic" and "commemorative" coins are collected for their scarcity value and often trade at a large and variable premium above their gold, silver, or platinum content value. Among the best known bullion coins are the South African gold Krugerrand, the American gold and silver Eagle coins, the Canadian gold, silver, and platinum Maple Leaf coins, and the Austrian gold Philharmonic.

bullion lead   an impure form of lead containing precious metals, other byproducts, and impurities.

byproduct   a secondary or additional metal or mineral produced by a mine or refinery in association with another metal. For example, silver is often produced as a byproduct of copper mining.

call or **call option**   a contract giving the buyer the right, but not the obligation, to purchase the underlying asset—such as mining equities or futures contracts—at a specified price (the strike price) on or before the specified date. The seller or grantor of the option is obligated to deliver the underlying asset if requested by the buyer. Upon entering into an options contract, the buyer pays the seller a fee or premium for the right to make the subsequent purchase.

cash production cost the cost of mining a given metal generally including milling, refining, and other direct production costs but usually excluding taxes, depreciation, financing, marketing and other indirect expenses. The exact definition may vary from one company to the next.

catalytic converter an automotive exhaust emission control device used to meet government imposed air pollution standards in many countries. These systems use platinum and/or palladium as the catalyst.

certificates a convenient vehicle for metals investors attesting to ownership of a specific quantity of the underlying metal that is held on behalf of the owner by a bank, brokerage house, or bullion dealer in a recognized depository or warehouse. Most often used by precious metals investors, certificates allow investors to avoid the costs of delivery and, where applicable, sales taxes.

clearinghouse an independent association responsible for matching up the buyers and sellers of futures contracts and options on organized exchanges (such as COMEX or the LME). The clearinghouse and its members or owners guarantee every contract traded on the relevant exchange and is responsible for collecting margin payments from all brokerage houses or traders doing business on the exchange. The clearinghouse assures the integrity and credibility of the exchange.

COMEX the Commodity Exchange, Inc. in New York City is the world's principal gold futures exchange which trades contracts representing future delivery of gold, silver, copper, and aluminum as well as options on gold and silver futures contracts.

Commodity Futures Trading Commission (CFTC) the U.S. government agency with responsibility for regulating American futures exchanges.

coinage bronze an alloy of 95 percent copper, 4 percent tin, and 1 percent zinc.

commemorative coins coins issued by a government to honor individuals or historic events. Usually these coins are minted in limited quantities and sold at a significant premium over their gold, silver, or other metal content value. Most often, commemoratives are legal tender of the issuing country and carry a face value well below both their metal content value and their initial selling price.

concentrate mine ore or other metal-containing material which has been treated to remove certain unwanted constituents prior to refining to produce metal of high purity.

contango originally a British term used on the stock exchange to describe a premium paid by the buyer of an equity for postponement transfer and payment to the next day. Contango now refers to the price relationship between the current or spot price of a metal and the higher price for future delivery. The magnitude of the contango does not normally exceed the cost of financing, insurance, and storage of the metal over the period until the delivery date.

coproducts metals that are mined together, both of which are valuable contributors to overall mine revenue.

covered call option if the writer or seller of a call option on metals, futures contracts, or equities owns the underlying asset and therefore can make delivery if required the option is covered. In contrast, a naked option is an option where the writer does not own the underlying asset.

cupro-nickel an alloy of approximately 70 percent copper and 30 percent nickel.

deficit in a metal market a shortage of total supply relative to industrial demand.

delivery date the specified date when a commodity traded on an exchange must be delivered to fulfill the terms of the futures contract.

depository a bank or other institution that stores metal on behalf of investors. A number of depositories are selected by a futures exchange as approved storage locations for metal that may be delivered against futures contracts. Often the term is used to refer to precious metals storage facilities while non-precious metals and other commodities traded on futures exchanges are held in warehouses.

dollar-cost averaging   see accumulation plans.

electroplating   the process by which a very fine coat of one metal, such as nickel, gold, or silver, is deposited on another metal by passing an electric current through a liquid solution between a cathode and an anode made of each metal, respectively.

exchange stocks   metal which is owned by futures market participants and which is held in exchange-approved warehouses or depositories. Exchange stocks are available for delivery against futures contracts.

exercise price   see strike price.

forward sale or **forward contract**   an agreement similar to a futures contract for the sale of a commodity on a specified future date at a pre-set price. Mining companies may sell forward in order to "lock in" or hedge the price they will receive when they deliver their metal production to the buyer.

fundamental analysis   see fundamentals and technical analysis.

fundamentals   the basic supply and demand position of a market. Fundamental analysis focuses on trends in supply and demand in contrast to technical analysis which studies past price and market action in order to predict future price trends.

futures contract   an agreement reached on the floor of an organized commodity futures exchange, such as the COMEX or NYMEX, calling for delivery of a specified quantity of metal (or other commodity) on a specified date in the future at an agreed upon price.

futures exchange   a membership association organized to facilitate the trading of futures contracts.

galvanizing   the application of a zinc coating to steel or other metals in order to prevent rusting and corrosion. Often the zinc coating is applied by dipping the steel in molten zinc or by electroplating.

gearing   see leverage.

good delivery or **good delivery bars**   metal that meets the standards of certain futures exchanges or market associations for delivery against short futures positions or to fulfill a physical sale. Good delivery metal must be cast by an approved refiner in an accepted weight and purity, all of which is stamped on the metal itself along with a serial number for identification.

grade   the metal content of ore or scrap usually defined in terms of grams, kilograms, or ounces per metric ton.

grantor   the seller or writer of an option.

gram   the basic unit of weight in the metric system. One kilogram equals 1000 grams. One gram equals 0.002083 troy ounces.

hedging   the use of various strategies often involving futures contracts, forward contracts, or options in order to offset the risk of price change in the marketplace. A mine can hedge against a possible decline in the price of its metal output by selling forward or buying put options.

hard lead   antimonial lead containing 5 to 15% antimony used for house gutters, roofing, and chemical tank linings.

ingot   a bar of gold, silver, or another metal.

in the money   a call option is said to be "in the money" when its strike price is lower than the current market price of the underlying asset. A put option is "in the money" when the strike price is above the current market price of the underlying asset.

intrinsic value   the amount by which an option is in the money. An option which is not in the money has no intrinsic value.

karat   a measure of gold's purity or fineness. 24 karat is pure gold of at least 99 percent fineness. 22 karat is an alloy containing 22 parts gold and 2 parts other metals. 14 karat is an alloy containing 14 parts gold and 10 parts other metals.

kerb trading   on the LME, a brief period at the end of each trading session when all of the listed metals are traded simultaneously. Originally, the term referred to off-exchange trading conducted literally on the curb of the street.

kilobar   a gold bar weighing exactly one kilogram or 32.1507 troy ounces.

lead bronze   an alloy of 2 to 10 percent tin, 15 to 32 percent lead, and 68 to 79 percent copper.

lead bullion   crude lead containing some silver.

leverage   in futures and options markets, the ability to control an investment the market value of which is a multiple of one's actual cash investment. Futures are leveraged because the investor pays only initial margin which is usually 5 or 10% of the contract's full value. Similarly, the premium paid on an option is only a fraction of the value of the underlying asset. Equities purchased on margin are leveraged for the same reason. However, in reference to equities—especially mining stocks—leverage may refer to the degree of price volatility of the stock price relative to the price of the metal or metals mined by the company. In Britain, Australia, and South Africa, this sensitivity of the stock price to the metal price is called gearing.

London Metal Exchange   the physical market in London, England—established in 1882—where a number of metals, including lead, copper, tin, aluminum—are traded. Also known as the LME, metals prices set by free and open trading on this exchange often serve as benchmark prices around the world.

malleability   the ability of a metal to be shaped without breaking, cracking, or rupture. Gold is the most malleable of all metals, a characteristic which makes the yellow metal exceptionally workable by jewelry fabricators and dentists.

margin   in futures markets, good faith funds put up as collateral to guarantee contract fulfillment. In equity markets, the partial payment, usually 50% of the stock purchase price, with the brokerage house lending its customers the balance.

margin call   a request from a broker for additional funds in order to raise the cash position back to minimum levels after an adverse price move on futures or equity markets.

metric ton or **tonne**   in the metric system, the unit of weight equal to 1000 kilograms or 32,150.7 troy ounces. A metric ton is equivalent to 2204.61 pounds.

naked option   see covered call option.

naval brass   an alloy of roughly 60 percent copper, roughly 40 percent zinc, and about 1 percent tin.

nonferrous metals   metals and alloys that do not contain iron or in which iron is only a minor constituent. Examples of nonferrous metals include copper, brass, bronze, tin, lead, aluminum, and zinc.

numismatic coins   coins which are valued by investors and collectors because of their rarity as well as their esthetic, cultural, or historical appeal rather than their metal content or face value. In contrast, bullion coins are valued only for their gold, silver, or platinum content.

NYMEX   the New York Mercantile Exchange in New York City is one of the world's principal platinum and palladium futures exchanges. NYMEX is also the leading exchange for oil and energy-related futures contracts.

open interest   on commodity futures or options markets, the number of outstanding contracts or positions which have not been offset or liquidated either by opposite transactions or by delivery of the underlying asset. Open interest is an important measure of market liquidity.

options   contracts giving the owner of the option the right but not the obligation to buy or sell an asset—such as a mining equity or futures contract. The grantor or writer of the option is obligated to buy or sell the underlying asset at a preset price upon demand by the option holder or owner. See also call, grantor, premium, put, strike price, and writer.

ore   a naturally occurring mineral that contains one or more metals or other elements in sufficient quantities and chemical combinations so that commercial mining and extraction can be profitable.

ore grade   usually reported in grams or kilograms per metric ton, is a measure of the metal content of a mine's orebody.

ore reserves   the amount of mineral bearing rock which can be exploited economically to yield metal or other minerals. Reserves are usually designated as proven, probable, possible, or potential, depending on the amount of quantifiable evidence available from drilling and other sampling to calculate estimated tonnage and mineral content.

out of the money   in options markets, refers to put options where the strike price is lower than the current market price of the underlying asset or call options where the strike price is higher than the current market price of the underlying asset.

pewterware   refers to kitchen and tabletop utensils, cookware, etc., fabricated from an alloy consisting of tin and also most frequently lead.

platinum group metal (PGM)   any of a number of related metals usually found in the same ore as coproducts or byproducts. In addition to platinum itself, the PGMs include palladium, rhodium, ruthenium, iridium, and osmium.

premium   for a bullion coin or bar, the difference between the price paid for the item and the current market value of its metal content. In the options market, the price paid by the buyer to the seller of the option.

price-earnings (P/E) ratio or **multiple**   a ratio in which a stock's current market price is divided by its past or prospective annual earnings. It is also a measure of the number of years it would take the company to earn its stock price.

primary supply   metal entering the market from mine production as opposed to scrap.

put or **put option**   a contract giving its buyer (the options holder) the right but not the obligation to sell an asset—such as mining equities, futures contracts, or physical metal—at a specified price (the strike price) on or before a specified date. The seller or grantor of the option is obligated to purchase the underlying asset if demanded by the option holder. Upon entering into an options contract, the holder pays the grantor a fee or premium for the right to make the subsequent sale.

pyramiding   the use of the appreciated value of futures contracts to finance the margin required for the acquisition of additional futures positions.

red brass   an alloy of 83 percent copper and 17 percent zinc used for casting, bearings, and valves.

refiner or **refinery**   a company or industrial complex that processes raw metals in order to separate the constituents of alloys and/or to remove impurities.

refining   the metallurgical process of upgrading and purifying minerals, metals, and industrial scrap into high-grade metal meeting acceptable industrial standards.

reserve life   a measure of the expected life of a mine, usually expressed in years, based upon the currently defined ore reserves and the planned or optimal rate of mine production.

reserves   see ore reserves.

ring   the official trading area on the floor of the London Metal Exchange.

scrap   metal-bearing material from old jewelry, industrial equipment, beverage cans, junked autos, for example, which is sent to a refiner or smelter in order to recover and recycle its metal content.

secondary supply   metal recovered from scrap which is refined and converted into bars or other acceptable "good delivery" forms and which is indistinguishable from primary supply once it enters the marketplace.

settlement price   often referred to as the closing price, this is the price set at the close of each trading day for every listed contract month on a futures exchange by the exchange's settlement committee. This price is the basis for determining margin calls by the clearinghouse.

smelter   a company or industrial complex that processes metal-bearing ores or scrap. See smelting.

smelting   a chemical reduction process of extracting raw metals, such as aluminum, from ores or concentrates by heat prior to refining into pure or high-grade metal.

solder   a metal alloy, often containing lead and/or tin, used to join two metals.

spot price   the price of a metal for immediate delivery in the physical market (usually 2 business days after the actual transaction date). In futures markets, spot refers to the price for the current delivery month.

stainless steel   alloy principally of steel and also frequently nickel which imparts a high resistance to rusting and corrosion.

storage account   a vehicle established by banks and brokerage houses allowing investors to make precious metals investments without taking delivery. Typically, the metal is held in a depository on behalf of the investor. Storage accounts are convenient mechanisms because they allow for easy purchase, resale, and storage. Like certificates, they also permit investors to avoid any state or local sales taxes.

sterling   silver of a standard purity consisting of 925 parts fine silver and 75 parts copper. Sterling is the typical purity of silver tableware, household items, and jewelry.

strike price   the predetermined contractual price at which an option may be exercised and the underlying asset bought (in the case of a call) or sold (in the case of a put). Also known as the exercise price.

surplus   in a metal market, a shortage of total supply relative to industrial demand.

technical analysis   the use of historical price, open interest, and volume statistics or charts to study an investment's past performance and forecast future price prospects. Technical analysis is preferred by some investors to fundamental analysis.

time value   the amount by which an option's premium exceeds its intrinsic value. Time value reflects the amount of time remaining before the option matures as well as the price volatility of the underlying asset.

troy ounce   a standard unit of weight commonly used for precious metals. One troy ounce equals 31.1034807 grams, 480 grains, or 20 pennyweights. 32.1507 troy ounces equals one kilogram.

warehouse and **warehouse receipts**   an exchange approved facility for holding metals or other commodities that are traded on a futures exchange. Warehouse receipts are issued representing ownership of the metal and satisfy an exchange's delivery requirements. See depository.

white gold   gold that has been alloyed with various combinations of platinum, palladium, nickel, copper, zinc, and/or silver to alter its color and hardness for jewelry applications, especially gem settings.

writer   see grantor.

yellow brass   an alloy of 70 percent copper and 30 percent zinc used for cartridge cases, condenser tubes, and so on.

yellow gold   an alloy of gold, silver, and copper (and sometimes zinc) intended to make the metal look yellower than natural gold.

yellow metal   a nickname or slang term for gold, used to distinguish it from the red metal (copper) or the white metals (platinum, palladium, or silver).

Index